AF505888

THE BOMB AND EUROPEAN SECURITY

THE BOMB
AND
EUROPEAN
SECURITY

by

GUIDO VIGEVENO

With a Foreword by
EUGENE V. ROSTOW

Indiana University Press
Bloomington

Manufactured in Great Britain

Library of Congress catalog card number: 83-48137
ISBN 0-253-31208-6 (cloth)
ISBN 0-253-21220-0 (paper)

FOREWORD

by Eugene V. Rostow

I am happy to commend Mr Guido Vigeveno's book, *The Bomb and European Security*, to serious readers on both sides of the ideological divide. It is a valuable popular analysis of the concept of deterrence, and most especially of the role of nuclear weapons in the dynamics of deterrence. Obviously, in the nuclear world, there can be no more important subject.

The notion of nuclear deterrence has changed since the beginning of the nuclear age in 1945. At first, optimists thought, the United States could cause the Soviet Union to desist from relatively minor aggression carried on by conventional forces, terror, or subversion simply by shaking a minatory finger and looking serious. It soon became apparent that this was not the case. Secretary Dulles' doctrine of 'massive retaliation' proved to be an empty threat. Secret nuclear hints were undoubtedly credible and helpful in bringing the Korean War to an end and in several other situations of crisis. But they were not convincing in Vietnam. And the problem we face now is to determine what our nuclear arsenal can really be expected to deter: only the possibility of attack on the United States itself? Conventional or only nuclear attack on NATO? On Japan as well? On China too? On other countries or vital interests?

Mr Vigeveno's study will permit his readers to confront these critical issues. While *The Bomb and European Security* is written in a NATO perspective, its icy, lucid, and well-informed chapters apply *mutatis mutandis* to the security problems of the world at large, and especially to those of Japan, Australia, New Zealand, China, South Korea, and the nations of the Middle East and other regions which must rely ultimately on the American nuclear guaranty.

Mr Vigeveno writes from the military point of view, and his concern is the credibility to the Soviet Union of American nuclear commitments, in view of the endless (and rapid) process of change in the nuclear balance, and in Soviet and American military doctrines about what nuclear weapons are for. The nuclear balance is being transformed both in numbers and in technological quality. Mr Vigeveno's disciplined account permits the reader to understand the significance of these changes both to the art of war and to world politics.

The Western policy of deterrence will not work at all, he demonstrates, unless Western armaments are sufficient to make any rational Soviet planner doubtful about the outcome of possible aggression. Deterrence, in short, is uncertainty. So long as the Soviet leaders believe that the American weapons could and might be used as a last resort, nuclear deterrence should continue to be effective, at least for the most vital interests of the United States, despite the relative success of the Soviet drive for nuclear superiority during the last decade or so.

If the United States fails to maintain a convincing retaliatory nuclear force — that is, a force convincing in this special sense — the Soviet Union will become capable of plausibly threatening aggression against Europe and other targets of central importance to the balance of power. Once such threats become manifest, the Soviet Union could reasonably believe that its nuclear arsenal is an immensely valuable *political* instrument of coercion, generating fundamental and irreversible changes in the foreign policies of all the Western nations.

For it cannot be said too often that the nuclear policy of the Soviet Union is not the Western nuclear policy of deterrence. It is altogether different. It views the nuclear weapon as the ultimate instrument of diplomatic blackmail — the sanction deterring any Western response to an endless campaign of expansion based on the use of conventional forces, terror, and subversion. As Mr Vigeveno's review of Soviet military doctrine confirms once again, the Soviet Union believes in the military philosophy of pre-emptive attack with all weapons, including the nuclear.

Armed with that formidable idea, the Soviet leaders have made the state of the military balance a powerful political influence. It is the source of currents of fear which are already transforming political positions all across the spectrum of Western politics. Parties of the Left, as we generally characterize political attitudes, are being riven by deep differences about how the West should respond to the threat implicit in

Soviet nuclear power. So are parties of the Right and Center. Some consider the conflict already lost, and advocate accommodation, unilateral disarmament, and surrender. A special form of that response is the revival of isolationism in the United States, where powerful and respected spokesmen are saying that great powers do not commit suicide for their allies; that no American President could now face a Soviet nuclear threat as President Kennedy did during the Cuban Missile Crisis, or as President Nixon did during the Yom Kippur War in 1973; and that therefore extended deterrence has become impossible.

These are absurd and unnecessary policies, manifesting only the impulse of *sauve-qui-peut* and the devil take the hindmost. But they must be taken seriously, and be overcome at all costs. For if these defeatist views gain much more ground, nuclear anxiety will turn into panic; the American alliance system will collapse; militarism, xenophobia, nuclear proliferation, and other contagious diseases will flourish; and the democratic world will disintegrate into impotence and defeat without a shot being fired. This outcome — defeat under the political pressure of what Soviet writers like to call 'the correlation of forces' — is a far more likely risk to the security and independence of the West than nuclear war for the decades ahead.

Mr Guido Vigeveno's book is a clear-headed introduction to this critical question — that is, whether it will continue to be possible for the United States to maintain a foreign policy based ultimately on the American nuclear umbrella or be forced back to isolation and neutrality in Fortress America. His answer to the question, with which I fully agree, is 'Yes, provided the United States and its allies do what is necessary to preserve extended deterrence in a changing military and political environment.'

Readers who are already expert in the field will read Mr Vigeveno's book with respect. Citizens who are concerned without being expert will find it a most useful and reliable guide.

Yale University
April 15, 1983

CONTENTS

Foreword by Eugene V. Rostow *page* v

Map: NATO and Warsaw Pact countries in Europe
and Soviet military districts   xii

1. Terminology   1

Strategic and tactical/theatre nuclear weapons   1
Eurostrategic and grey area   4
New terminology   5

2. NATO Strategy   7

Former strategy: massive retaliation   7
Present strategy: flexible response   8
Deterrence   12
Defence   17
The role of tactical nuclear weapons in NATO
   strategy   18
Crisis management and escalation control   21
Nuclear release procedures   23

3. Soviet Strategy   25

Attitude towards nuclear and chemical weapons   27
The offensive   29
Political decision-making   32
(No) first use   33
Theatre warfare   35

4. The Military Balance   38

The conventional balance   40
The strategic nuclear balance   42
The theatre nuclear balance: problems of analysis   44
Warsaw Pact nuclear forces affecting the balance in
   land theatres   45
NATO nuclear forces affecting the balance in land
   theatres   48
Qualitative and quantitative shifts in the balance   50
The maritime balance   53
Implications for NATO strategy   55

5. Arms Control and Disarmament   59

     From SALT to START   66
     MBFR   71

6. Refinements of US/NATO Strategy   75

     'Pure deterrence' versus 'deterrence through defence'   76

7. The Neutron Bomb   80

     Technical features   80
     Tactical implications   82
     Strategic implications   82
     The nuclear threshold   83
     Production decision   85

8. Armament and Disarmament in the Grey Area   88

     The dual-track approach   89
     The Soviet campaign against the presence of
       American nuclear weapons in Europe   94
     Positions of Western protagonists   95
     The arms control track   101

Appendix: Tables and Charts   120

PLATES

(between pages 36–37)

Presidents Carter and Brezhnev at the signing of the SALT II Treaty, Vienna, June 1979.
The INF negotiators in Geneva.
Yuri Andropov.
The Prague summit, January 1983.
A Soviet 'Scud' missile.
The Soviet SS–20 (artist's impression).
The Soviet 'Backfire' bomber carrying a cruise missile.
Two Soviet 'Badger' bombers.
A Soviet *Juliett* class cruise missile submarine.
A US ground-launched cruise missile.
The US 'Pershing' II missile.
Soviet SA–2 'Guideline' missiles.
The US aircraft-carrier *Forrestal*.
Cartoon from *Het Parool*, Amsterdam.

Iceland
Siberia
Ural
Leningrad
Norway
Volga
Denmark
Baltic
Moscow
United Kingdom
Belorussia
Central Asia
Netherlands
GDR
Poland
Belgium
Luxembourg
Federal Republic of Germany
CSSR
Carpathian
Kiev
North Caucasus
France
Hungary
Odessa
Portugal
Spain
Italy
Rumania
Trans Caucasus
Bulgaria
Turkey
Greece
NATO AND WARSAW PACT COUNTRIES IN EUROPE
AND SOVIET MILITARY DISTRICTS

1

TERMINOLOGY

Strategic and tactical/theatre nuclear weapons

Nuclear weapons are regarded as *strategic* if they are intended for use either against urban and industrial centres, or against military objectives essential to the enemy's overall war effort. An attack against urban and/or industrial targets is referred to as a 'counter-city' or 'counter-value' strike. An attack against military targets is known as a 'counter-force' strike.

Strategic nuclear assets are included among military targets considered essential to the enemy's overall war effort.

Tactical nuclear weapons are those intended for use against military targets (conventional or nuclear) which are more directly related to the battlefield itself. The nature of the objective is the main factor determining whether an attack is tactical or strategic. Another factor is the location of the objective. Tactical nuclear weapons would be used primarily in the combat area, for instance against enemy units, and further to the rear against reinforcements, lines of communication, command and control centres and airfields.

Strategic nuclear weapons would be directed against targets in the heart of the enemy's territory, and therefore have a longer range than the tactical ones. In general they also have a much greater destructive power, though this is not always so. In fact, it is not so much the intrinsic features of a weapon which may be termed tactical or strategic, but rather the way it is used. The line between the two concepts is often blurred. Several weapons can be used in both a tactical and a strategic role.

The strategic nuclear forces of the United States consist of 'Intercontinental Ballistic Missiles' (ICBMs), long-range heavy bombers and 'Submarine-Launched Ballistic Missiles' (SLBMs). This is often termed 'the triad'. The ICBMs have a range of over 11,000 km., which enables them to reach any part of the Soviet Union from their protective silos in the

United States. Long-range bombers have a combat radius[1] of about 8,000 km., which is sufficient to enable round trip missions to be made deep into Soviet territory. The range of current American SLBMs is about 4,600 km., which enables them to reach the Soviet Union from submarines cruising in the open sea. The Soviet Union has similar weapon systems. In addition, it has strategic defensive forces including an anti-ballistic missile (ABM) system around Moscow and an extensive air defence network throughout its territory.

ICBMs, SLBMs and heavy bombers are often called 'central systems'.

Other systems, i.e. those that are not central, belong to a 'theatre of operations' — i.e. a geographical area where ground, air and naval operations are co-ordinated to some degree. In the event of a world-wide armed conflict between East and West, the whole of Europe and the adjacent seas are likely to be involved; this would constitute the European theatre of operations. There might also be other theatres, for example in the Far East.

The term 'Theatre Nuclear Forces' (TNF) denotes all the nuclear assets in a given theatre or at the disposal of the military commander in charge of that area. In the European theatre, the regional commander for NATO — the North Atlantic Treaty Organisation — is called SACEUR ('Supreme Allied Commander Europe').

In traditional military terminology, *tactical* denotes that which pertains to lower-level operations. As some tactical nuclear delivery systems can cover a distance of more than 1,000 km., the term *Theatre Nuclear Forces* is often used for the sake of greater clarity. In fact 'tactical nuclear' and 'theatre nuclear' both refer to the same category of nuclear forces.

The United Kingdom has four 'Polaris' ballistic missile submarines. They are assigned to SACEUR, but the British government has reserved the right to use them independently when 'supreme national interests are at stake'. The 'Polaris' force clearly constitutes the ultimate national deterrent and

---

1. The combat radius of an aircraft is usually somewhat less than half its unrefuelled range.

should therefore be considered strategic, even though it is in fact based in the European theatre and could be used in reaction to a Soviet attack with, say, SS–20 missiles. The British regard the rest of their nuclear capabilities as an integral part of NATO's Theatre Nuclear Forces.

France is a member of the Alliance, but does not participate in its integrated military structure. French nuclear forces are not therefore taken into account by NATO nuclear planning. The French regard their larger systems (ballistic missile submarines, land-based intermediate-range ballistic missiles and intermediate-range bombers) as strategic and their smaller systems as tactical.

Instead of the familiar two-tier distinction between tactics and strategy, Soviet military planners use a three-tier approach. They consider as *tactical* all operations by units of division size or smaller. The standard nuclear weapon at the disposal of a division commander in Warsaw Pact forces is the 'Frog', a rocket with a range of about 70 km. The 'army' and the 'front' (consisting of 4–7 armies[2]) form the *operational* level. At these two levels we find 'Scud' and 'Scaleboard' missiles respectively (the first with a range of 300 km. and the second with a range of 900 km.). Military operations above the 'front' level, i.e. those which are theatre-wide or world-wide, are regarded as *strategic*. All missiles with a range above

2. Warsaw Pact military organisation does not correspond to that of NATO. The respective personnel strength of the main formations and units is given below. A unit normally comprises 3–5 sub-units (e.g. an American division comprises three brigades).

NATO

battalion	500–900
brigade	3,000–5,000
division	12,000–16,000
army corps	50,000–80,000
army group, e.g. NORTHAG (Northern Army Group Central Europe), which comprises four army corps	

Warsaw Pact

battalion	200–450
regiment	1,000–2,200
division	10,000–12,000
army	60,000–80,000
front	4–7 armies

1,000 km. form part of the 'Strategic Rocket Forces', a separate service in the Soviet Union.

Eurostrategic and grey area

In 1969 the United States and the Soviet Union began 'Strategic Arms Limitations Talks' (SALT). These arms control talks were initially devoted exclusively to the strategic weaponry of the two superpowers. For the purposes of the talks, any nuclear delivery system which could clearly reach the territory of one superpower from the territory of the other was defined as strategic (the shortest distance being 5,500 km.). In addition, all SLBMs on board nuclear-powered submarines were considered to be strategic. In the course of the SALT II negotiations (1973–9), the Soviet Union started deploying systems like the 'Backfire' bomber and the SS–20 missile, which did not quite fit the SALT definition of strategic but which were nevertheless of strategic importance, especially for Western Europe. This drew attention to the fact that, whereas for Americans only weapon systems with an intercontinental range were strategic, for Europeans systems with a far shorter range could clearly have a strategic significance. Hence the term 'Eurostrategic' came into being.

At the same time, arms control experts grew worried that SALT II would be circumvented, even before it was signed, by the development of cruise missiles in the United States and the introduction of the 'Backfire' and SS–20 by the Soviet Union. This was to become known as the 'grey area', and consisted of a whole new family of weapons, which escaped all current attempts at arms control. Some US medium-range theatre nuclear systems were being discussed at the time in the MBFR (Mutual Balanced Force Reductions) talks in Vienna, but there was no arms control forum in which long-range theatre nuclear forces were being addressed in any systematic fashion. In the end, however, the SALT II treaty did contain some limitations on cruise missiles as well as on 'Backfire' production (see pp. 67–8).

The grey area can no longer be viewed as a gap in the arms control efforts, since negotiations on such systems have started in Geneva. However the grey area concept may still be of some use to denote the category of weapons that forms the transition between the tactical and the strategic. Ambiguity

characterises the grey area weapons. Within a given theatre
they can be employed for tactical as well as strategic missions,
and a system like the 'Backfire' is even capable of performing
intercontinental missions under certain circumstances.

New terminology

The concept of a theatre can sometimes give rise to confusion
too, because people tend to equate it with existing geographic
boundaries, which are not necessarily significant in a military
sense. A case in point is the 5,000 km.-range SS–20, which can
easily reach targets in Western Europe from locations well to
the east of the Urals. Such considerations have prompted the
elaboration of a new terminology, which focusses on range
criteria:

CLASSICAL NATO TERMINOLOGY

1. Strategic Nuclear Forces
2. Theatre Nuclear Forces (TNF)
    (*a*) Long-Range Theatre Nuclear Forces (LRTNF)
    (between 1,000/1,500 and 5,500 km.)
    (*b*) Medium-Range Theatre Nuclear Forces (MRTNF)
    (between 150 and 1,000/1,500 km.)
    (*c*) Short-Range Theatre Nuclear Forces (SRTNF),
    also referred to as battlefield systems
    (up to about 150 km.)
    (*d*) Maritime or sea-based nuclear forces
3. Conventional forces

NEW NATO TERMINOLOGY

1. Strategic Nuclear Forces
2. Non-strategic or "other" nuclear forces
    (*a*) Intermediate-Range Nuclear Forces (INF)
    — Longer-Range INF missiles
        (between 1,800 and 5,500 km.)
    — Shorter-Range INF missiles
        (between $\pm$ 150 and 1,800 km.)
    — INF aircraft

(*b*) Short-Range Nuclear Forces (SNF)
(up to ± 150 km.)
(*c*) Maritime or sea-based nuclear forces
3. Conventional forces

This new terminology is increasingly being used in official presentations.

2
NATO STRATEGY

At the end of the Second World War, the Red Army occupied the eastern half of Europe. Stalin seized the opportunity offered to him by history to push the Soviet border westward and to bring the East European countries under his control by putting local communist parties into power. As the Red Army had been only partially demobilised, unlike the Western armies, it enjoyed overwhelming superiority on the continent. Many feared at that time that after achieving control over Eastern Europe, the Soviet Union would try through either overt or covert means to extend its influence to Western Europe. In 1947 the United States introduced the Marshall Plan, which helped the war-torn economies of the West European countries to recover. In 1949 the United States formally committed itself to the defence of Western Europe through the North Atlantic Treaty, thereby restoring something of a balance on the continent. The Soviet Union maintained much larger ground forces, but the United States enjoyed a near-monopoly in nuclear weapons. To this day, although things have of course changed since the early days of the Cold War when NATO came into being, the American nuclear guarantee remains the cornerstone of the Alliance and the basis of European security.

Former strategy: massive retaliation

During the first years of its existence, NATO endeavoured to build a conventional force capable of withstanding a Soviet invasion. By 1954 it had become clear that the European members of the Alliance, even with North American help, would not be able to carry the burden of maintaining an adequate conventional defence. The Alliance therefore based its strategy on the nuclear supremacy which the United States enjoyed at the time. Any kind of aggression, it was proclaimed, would automatically lead to massive nuclear retaliation. The strategy of 'massive retaliation', as it was called, was designed to remove any temptation on the part of the Soviet leadership to exploit in some way its massive conventional preponderance on the continent.

The strategy maximised deterrence. Moreover, it had a big practical advantage: because it removed the need for large conventional forces, it was relatively cheap. The role of conventional forces was merely that of a 'trip-wire' or 'shield'. As soon as it was touched, the nuclear sword would be drawn.

Gradually the Soviet Union acquired the means of delivering nuclear weapons of its own. In 1955 it brought in the first bomber of continental range, and a year later the first intercontinental bomber. So the West was now becoming vulnerable to nuclear attack. As the Soviet Union built up its nuclear strength, the threat of massive retaliation became less credible.

While the United States still enjoyed a near-monopoly of nuclear weapons and means of delivery, it had already refrained from using or even threatening to use nuclear weapons in contingencies like the Berlin blockade and the invasion of South Korea. It became even more unlikely that the United States would respond to limited challenges of this nature or to small incursions into NATO territory with massive nuclear strikes against Soviet cities, now that the Soviet Union was able to do just the same. It was also becoming apparent that in the event of a conflict with the Soviet Union, lack of conventional forces could place NATO only too rapidly in the dilemma of having either to surrender or to initiate mutual suicide.

Present strategy: flexible response

In 1962, realising that the trip-wire strategy was either no longer credible or risked setting the world ablaze over a minor border conflict in Europe or elsewhere, the US Secretary of Defense, Robert McNamara, developed a new strategy. Unlike the massive retaliation concept, which provided only for a single — massive — response to the various possible forms of aggression, the new strategy offered the possibility of choice; hence the name 'strategy of flexible response'.

The conventional shield now took on fresh importance,

while the nuclear sword became a weapon to be used only in the last resort. Consistent with its new doctrine, the United States started strengthening its conventional capabilities and asked its Allies to follow suit.

The turn-about in American strategic thinking caused a temporary crisis of confidence within the Alliance. The Europeans feared that the Americans were in fact trying to close the nuclear umbrella they had been holding over them until then. The abandonment of the massive retaliation strategy confirmed General de Gaulle in his view that the United States was not to be relied upon, and contributed to his decision in 1966 to withdraw France from NATO's integrated military structure. The other European members of the Alliance finally came round to the new strategy, which was formally agreed upon in 1967, after some modifications had been made to the concept which the United States had originally proposed. It has held good to this day.

The strategy of flexible response, as adopted in 1967, constitutes a broad overall political and military concept for the defence of the Alliance. Of course, strategic thinking has not stood still since that date, and refinements were made to the concept in the course of the 1970s, as described in Chapter 6.

The fundamental objective of NATO's present as well as former strategy is to preserve peace and to ensure the security of the Allies by deterring any form of aggression. Should deterrence nevertheless fail and aggression against one or more of the Allies occur, NATO will have to defend itself with the aim of restoring its territorial integrity and re-establishing an effective deterrence. The objectives of the Alliance are strictly defensive; it would never be the first to take up arms. As the heads of state and government of the NATO countries declared at Bonn on 10 June 1982, 'None of our weapons will ever be used except in response to attack.'

The Soviet Union has the means to initiate — with or without the support of the other members of the Warsaw Pact — a variety of actions against NATO countries. These range from subversion and attempts at coercion to outright aggression. The flexible response strategy is designed to match the various possible forms of pressure and aggression with a comparable diversity of means for riposte. This enables NATO to adapt its response to the level of aggression and avoid unnecessary escalation. In order to implement its strategy, NATO needs military capabilities across the entire spectrum of conflict possibilities, i.e. conventional, tactical nuclear and strategic nuclear weapons.

If for instance conventional Warsaw Pact forces were to cross the border, NATO could first try to repel them with conventional means alone, in what is called *direct defence*. If the defenders succeed in bringing the offensive to a halt, the onus of escalation rests with the attacker. Should its conventional defences be overrun, NATO then has the option of deliberately raising the scope and intensity of the conflict. If all types of conventional weapons have already been engaged, one such step would be to resort to a carefully controlled use of tactical nuclear weapons, aimed at driving home to the invader the determination of the Allies to resist aggression and thereby induce him to cease hostilities and withdraw.

NATO strategy does not exclude the possibility of *deliberate escalation* — including nuclear weapons — when deemed necessary. In fact it is this possibility of escalation which forms the essence of deterrence. Although NATO would strive to restore its territorial integrity and security as soon as possible and with as little violence as possible, it can not be excluded that a conventional conflict would lead to the use of tactical nuclear weapons, which could in turn lead to the use of strategic weapons. These incalculable risks, which far outweigh any possible benefits a potential aggressor might hope to gain, should remove any possible expansionist inclination he might have harboured. Although it is possible to think of all kinds of scenarios in which nuclear weapons might be used — indeed the drawing up of contingency plans is part of the normal work of military staffs — there is really no way whereby anybody can predict with confidence how such events would actually develop. The uncertainty that surrounds any use of nuclear weapons is a major element of deterrence.

Naturally it would be greatly preferable if NATO had sufficient conventional forces to ensure that any conventional attack could be met by similar means alone. Unfortunately the European countries are not prepared to carry the burden of sufficiently large conventional forces. The price they have to pay is a heavier reliance on nuclear deterrence.

The communiqué of the May 1975 meeting of the Defence Planning Committee summarised NATO strategy as follows:

> The aim of NATO's strategy and military planning is to ensure security through deterrence. The primary aim is to deter an attack before it is launched, by making it clear to any aggressor that any attack on NATO would be met by a strong defence and might initiate a sequence of events which cannot be calculated in advance, involving risks to the aggressor out of all proportion to any advantages he might hope to gain. In an era of broad strategic nuclear parity, deterrence to all forms of aggression cannot be based upon strategic nuclear forces alone; it must be provided by the overall capabilities of all NATO forces. The Alliance must be able to respond in an appropriate manner to aggression of any kind; the response must be effective in relation to the level of force used by the aggressor and must at the same time make him recognise the dangers of escalation to a higher level.
>
> Should aggression occur, the military aim is to preserve or restore the integrity and security of the NATO area by employing such forces as may be necessary within the concept of forward defence and flexibility in response. NATO forces must be prepared to use any capabilities at their disposal (including nuclear weapons) for this purpose. This determination must be evident to the aggressor.

As has already been indicated, NATO in order to implement its strategy of flexible response, needs a 'triad' of conventional, tactical nuclear and strategic nuclear forces. The United States provides most of the nuclear forces, whereas the other Allies provide the greater part of the conventional forces.

An important requirement, especially with regard to nuclear forces, is that they be structured in such a way as to generate stability. It would be highly dangerous, for example, if each side were able to eliminate all the nuclear assets of the other in one strike (this is called a 'first strike capability'), since both would then have a strong incentive to strike first.

Nuclear weapons are therefore needed in sufficient numbers and with a sufficient degree of invulnerability to be able, even after sustaining a first strike, to inflict unacceptable damage upon an enemy. This is called a 'second strike capability'. For many years now, both superpowers have possessed a second strike capability, thus contributing to a stable strategic relationship — the so-called 'balance of terror' or 'mutual assured destruction'. The seaborne leg of the American and Soviet strategic arsenals, consisting of ballistic missile submarines, is least vulnerable and therefore plays an important role in maintaining a secure retaliatory capacity.

Mutual assured destruction has been compared to the predicament of two scorpions in a bottle: a fight would be bound to end in death for both of them. To avoid this, they manoeuvre very carefully. Mutual assured destruction has no doubt had a restraining influence on superpower behaviour. However, it does not on its own provide a sufficient safeguard, because it is not likely to deter smaller-scale challenges, such as limited conventional incursion.

Although primarily applicable to strategic nuclear forces, the concept of a second strike capability also has a bearing on theatre nuclear forces, because they too can be the subject of a surprise attack.

Deterrence

The prime objective of NATO strategy is to prevent war through deterrence. Deterrence is in fact a warning, directed at any potential aggressor. The effectiveness of this warning depends on:
1. the size and structure of NATO military capabilities;
2. the will actually to use these capabilities if it becomes necessary; and
3. a potential aggressor's perception of both of the above.
The third point needs particular emphasis. For NATO the aim of deterrence is to influence the calculations of the Soviet leaders. Its defence capability and resolve should therefore be clearly visible. If deterrence is to work, it must be credible. Doubts as to the West's capacity or will to defend itself could lead the Soviet leadership to dangerous miscalculations, such

as occurred during the Cuban missile crisis.

In 1962 Khrushchev had SS–4 and SS–5 medium-range missiles deployed in Cuba. The missiles were clearly aimed at the United States. It seems that the Soviet leader did not think that John F. Kennedy, the young American President, would dare to oppose this, but contrary to his expectations, Kennedy ordered the US Navy to impose a quarantine on the island. Soviet ships with additional missiles were on their way. For a few edgy days the two superpowers faced each other; then Khrushchev backed down. He ordered his ships to turn round and agreed to dismantle the missile base in Cuba. No doubt the preponderance of American naval power in the area and the overall strategic superiority the United States enjoyed at that time had an important influence on the outcome of the confrontation.

The possibility of escalation is a basic element of deterrence. To make the threat of escalation credible, however, NATO military capabilities have to 'interlock' across the full spectrum of conflict possibilities. It is not very convincing to affirm that you are willing to climb a ladder if several rungs are visibly either missing or loose. The lack of intermediate options was in fact the main weakness of the strategy of massive retaliation. Crucial to the system of interlocking deterrents is the link between the strategic weapons in the United States or at sea, on the one hand, and the TNF based in Europe, on the other. It expresses the willingness of the Americans to run the risk of a nuclear conflict spreading to their homeland for the defence of Europe. If the NATO force structure showed a gap between the TNF based in Europe and the American strategic forces, the Soviets might come to believe — however wrongly — that they could use tactical nuclear weapons against Western Europe without running any serious risk of damage to their own country. The American commitment has been reaffirmed time and again by successive administrations. The US Defense Secretary Harold Brown, addressing the Senate Foreign Relations Committee on 19 September 1979 on the recurring doubts among Europeans over the US commitment to their defence, had the following to say:

'To put this issue in historical perspective, I would note that it is a concern that has surfaced periodically in our relations with our Allies . . .

'Let me state quite clearly for all to hear — including those in Europe and this country who should know better but still tend to question our commitment to the defence of Europe: the United States is committed to the security and integrity of Western Europe, not only because it is in the interest of Europe but because it is in the vital interest of the United States. This has been the fundamental bedrock of US national security policy since at least 1947 and arguably since 1917.

'This is our policy because any threat to Western Europe is a threat not only to our cultural and intellectual roots but a vital threat to our economic, political and military security. This has been our policy. It is our policy. And we have and will continue to have the military means to secure that objective. In particular, the commitment of US central strategic forces to NATO security remains valid. President Carter reaffirmed that commitment early in his administration: "Let there be no misunderstanding. The US is prepared to use all the forces necessary for the defence of the NATO areas."

'Parity has not changed the validity of that commitment. It has never been a commitment free of risk, and ever since the Soviet Union acquired substantial and survivable nuclear forces, those risks have been great indeed. Not for decades has America's commitment to Europe depended on — or enjoyed the luxury of — an ability to limit to low levels the damage to the United States from an all-out Soviet attack.

'It is a grim but inescapable aspect of nuclear reality that in the nuclear era deterrence depends much more on our ability to use nuclear weapons to impose losses on an enemy, than on our ability to limit damage to ourselves. There are, of course, great uncertainties about what would happen if nuclear weapons were used. No one can be confident in his predictions how a nuclear exchange would evolve. Indeed, this uncertainty, coupled with the horrible results sure to follow from maximum escalation, is an essential element of deterrence.'

Confronted with the mistaken belief in some areas of European public opinion that the United States would rather fight a prolonged nuclear battle in Europe than put its own territory at risk, President Reagan reasserted:

'The suggestion that the United States could even consider fighting a nuclear war at Europe's expense is an outright deception. The essence of United States nuclear strategy is that no aggressor should believe that the use of nuclear weapons in Europe could reasonably be limited to Europe. Indeed, it is the joint European-American commitment to share the burden of our common defence, which assures the peace. Thus, we regard any military threat to Europe as a threat to the United States itself. 375,000 United States servicemen provide the living guarantee of this unshakable United States commitment to the peace and security of Europe.'[3]

If it is legitimate for the Europeans to demand a full commitment from the United States, it is equally legitimate for the United States to ask its European allies to share the nuclear burden and the risks involved. Allied solidarity is a two-way street. To demonstrate the indivisibility of Alliance security and to share nuclear responsibility, the United States stockpiled nuclear weapons on European soil and provided its European partners with tactical nuclear launchers.

Solidarity between NATO members, epitomised by the assertion that 'an armed attack against one or more of them in Europe or North America shall be considered an attack against them all',[4] is essential for maintaining effective deterrence across the whole of NATO territory. The fact that nuclear weapons are deployed on both sides of the Atlantic gives tangible form to the close link between the defence of Europe and that of the United States, and symbolises the willingness of Allies to share risks.

Understandably, it is in the nuclear field that Allied solidarity is most difficult to maintain. Each NATO country, given the choice, would no doubt prefer to leave the nuclear

3. 21 October 1981.
4. See Article V of the North Atlantic Treaty, 1949.

part of the common defence to the others, in the vain hope that by so doing it would run less risk in the event of war. The Soviet Union plays upon these natural feelings by inciting European countries to refuse American nuclear weapons on their soil with the promise of sparing them in the case of a nuclear conflict. Of course such promises offer no real guarantee whatsoever, since Soviet capabilities remain unaffected. In fact it is quite unlikely that if, say, the Netherlands and Belgium were to become nuclear-free, this would keep the Soviets from launching their missiles against vital harbours like Rotterdam and Antwerp, if they considered such an action necessary to prevent reinforcements from disembarking there.

It should also be noted that the presence of nuclear weapons in Western Europe is needed to dissuade Soviet leaders from exploiting in any way their conventional preponderance on the continent. As long as the conventional imbalance remains, NATO cannot afford to renounce either the deployment of nuclear weapons in Europe or the option of being the first to cross the nuclear threshold in reaction to a massive onslaught with conventional forces.

The British and French nuclear forces strengthen the overall deterrent. Their value lies not so much in their size, which is small in relation to the superpowers, but in the fact that London and Paris constitute independent centres of decision. This increases the uncertainty facing any Soviet leader contemplating some action against Western Europe, and hedges against any Soviet misperception concerning US resolve.

In the foregoing, emphasis has been placed on the need for the whole range of tactical and strategic nuclear weapons to form a closely interlocking continuum. There is one point, however, where it is desirable to maintain a clear break in the spectrum, namely between conventional and nuclear warfare. To cross the nuclear threshold is, in the NATO philosophy, a step of far-reaching political consequences, which would only be taken in extreme circumstances after most careful thought and undoubtedly painstaking deliberations. In military terms it is considered a qualitative jump of dramatic proportions. It follows that conventional and nuclear weapons should remain clearly distinguishable as to their effects. The manufacture of weapons which would blur the threshold between conventional and nuclear warfare, such as 'mininukes', has been categorically rejected by NATO.

Defence

If deterrence fails and aggression takes place, the Allies will have to defend themselves and repel the attack so as restore their territorial integrity. They would put up such resistance as would be necessary to induce the assailant to halt his attack and withdraw.

Deterrence and defence are in fact two sides of the same coin. The better NATO is able to frustrate the aggressor's ambitions through direct defence, the stronger deterrence will be. This has sometimes been termed deterrence by *denial*. As an insurance against a possible failure of direct defence, NATO has the means to deter through *punishment*, i.e. with nuclear weapons, especially the strategic ones.

Since the Federal Republic of Germany became a member of the Alliance in 1955, NATO has incorporated the concept of 'forward defence' into its strategy. This means that NATO forces will strive to halt an invasion as soon as possible, and as near to the border with the countries of the Warsaw Pact as possible. The concept of forward defence flows primarily from *political* considerations: it underlines the principle that all parts of NATO territory are considered equally worth defending and expresses the determination of the Allies not to tolerate any infringement of their borders. The alternative — defence in depth — would entail trading space for time in the opening stage of a conflict. Such a proposition is clearly unacceptable to the West Germans as it would involve the sacrifice of a large part of the territory of the Federal Republic.

Militarily speaking, a forward defence is called for because the space between the inner German border and the North Sea is already cramped. A second military argument is that the more territory is yielded initially in accordance with the doctrine of elastic defence, the more territory NATO would later have to reconquer in order to restore its territorial integrity. This reconquest might prove very difficult.

NATO strategy is purely defensive, in contrast to Soviet strategy which is not, as will be seen in the next chapter. The Alliance has forsworn the option to initiate hostilities, even if there were strong indications of an impending Warsaw Pact attack. The option of a 'pre-emptive' attack, designed to forestall an enemy attack, has thus been ruled out. The initiative is left to the adversary.

The defensive orientation of the Alliance is reflected in its military posture. Allied ground forces have neither the size nor the structure to conduct offensive operations into Warsaw Pact territory. The openness of Western societies makes it easy for the Soviets to see for themselves that NATO has neither the intention nor the capability to conquer Warsaw Pact territory. In military terms they have therefore no reason whatsoever to fear the West. In fact many analysts even doubt whether NATO has sufficient forces to fulfil its purely defensive purpose, if the need for it to do so were to arise.

The role of tactical nuclear weapons in NATO strategy

The chief purpose of tactical nuclear weapons is, like that of all nuclear weapons, to deter.

Under normal peacetime conditions NATO Theatre Nuclear Forces fulfil the following functions:
— to deter a conventional attack (in conjunction with conventional forces);
— to deter a potential aggressor from using his own tactical nuclear weapons;
— to provide a link between conventional forces in Europe and US strategic nuclear forces, which lends credibility to the declared readiness to escalate to the highest level of violence if necessary;
— to demonstrate Allied solidarity and cohesion in a tangible way through the participation of European NATO members in the manning and maintenance of delivery vehicles, thereby strengthening overall deterrence.

Once conventional warfare has broken out, NATO's TNF complicate the enemy's conventional operations and force him to disperse his troops. Once the decision to cross the nuclear threshold has been taken, NATO's TNF provide a means of deliberately raising the costs and risks of aggression short of all-out nuclear war, with the aim of restoring deterrence. Thus it can be seen that deterrence operates simultaneously at different levels. TNF deter the adversary from the use of both conventional and tactical nuclear weapons.

Deterrence can also fail at one level of violence while continuing to work at a higher level. The Second World War provides a good example. Although Hitler did not hesitate to initiate conventional warfare, he refrained throughout the war from using chemical weapons, because he knew that the Allies had the capacity to retaliate. Some analysts describe this as 'intra-war deterrence'. In the present-day context one could, for example, conceive that an aggressor would refrain from engaging all the conventional means at his disposal, lest this would spark off a tactical nuclear response.

Finally it is important to mention in this connection the possibility of restoring deterrence (entirely or partly) after hostilities have taken place. Such a result would be achieved if the aggressor ceased all hostilities following the use of TNF by NATO.

The special contribution of TNF to overall deterrence lies in the fact that they constitute the intermediate rungs on the ladder of violence. TNF are less formidable than strategic forces, but more formidable than conventional ones.

At present, the strategic arsenals of the two superpowers are roughly equivalent. This means that whatever escalatory steps the Americans might take, the Soviets can repay them in kind or worse. In such a situation it is no longer credible to proclaim, as in the 1950s, that a conventional attack would elicit a massive nuclear response. Hence the need for less suicidal options. Under the former NATO strategy, TNF were seen as a complement to the strategic forces, designed to neutralise the invading forces while the strategic sword struck at the heart of the enemy. In the present strategy, TNF constitute an intermediate phase that might have to be passed through in order to demonstrate resolve, but in which one hopes that it would also be possible to reverse the escalation process, thus avoiding an all-out nuclear war.

As was mentioned at the outset, the willingness of Europeans to share the risks and responsibilities of nuclear deterrence is demonstrated in a tangible manner through their participation in TNF. Following a decision of the North Atlantic Council in 1957, the United States started providing tactical nuclear launchers to their Allies. The warheads for these launchers are stored in Europe but remain under American control.

An important function fulfilled by the mere presence of tactical nuclear weapons, especially those with a shorter range, is to complicate the enemy's planning and force him to adopt less effective tactics than he would otherwise have chosen. Because NATO forces are equipped with tactical nuclear weapons, the commanders of an invading force would constantly have to reckon with the possibility that these weapons would be used against them. Normally an attacker can be expected to concentrate his troops against a few points of the defences to try and break through. Such concentrations would form easy targets for short-range nuclear weapons, and therefore commanders would be obliged to keep their troops more dispersed. This would facilitate the task of the defenders, who would be faced with less concentrated attacks and whose chances of being able to hold on without actually having to resort to nuclear weapons would thereby be increased.

In order to perform their deterrent function both before and during a conflict and to prevent enemy concentrations, TNF have to be militarily effective. The defence function of TNF wholly supports TNF's deterrent and preventive functions. The defence function takes varied forms:
— Short-range, battlefield support systems can destroy the leading elements of an invading force.
— Medium-range TNF (shorter-range INF in the new terminology) can be used against second-echelon targets, lines of communication, airfields etc.
— Long-range TNF (longer-range INF in the new terminology) can strike at rear area targets, including those in the Soviet Union itself (airfields, missile sites etc.).
— Other categories of tactical nuclear systems are designed to destroy aircraft, warships or even submarines.

Although the deterrent function of TNF could not be performed by conventional weapons because of the fundamental differences between the two, it is feasible that some of the TNF defence functions could in the future be taken over by new conventional systems. Technological progress, notably in the field of precision guidance, may make it possible for certain tasks to be performed with conventional means which at present can only be done with nuclear weapons. This would open the way for the withdrawal of certain types of tactical nuclear weapons.

Crisis management and escalation control

The concepts of 'crisis management' and 'escalation control' are refinements of the overall NATO strategy of flexible response intended to preserve peace and maintain the independence and territorial integrity of member-nations. The first concept applies to situations short of war; the second applies to actual war situations.

Crisis management can be described as the whole range of co-ordinated diplomatic, economic, military and other efforts aimed at solving an international crisis or at least preventing it from escalating into an armed conflict, without sacrificing the vital interests involved.

Escalation control can be described as the whole range of co-ordinated efforts, including escalatory and de-escalatory measures, aimed at terminating an armed conflict as soon as possible with as little violence as possible, under terms compatible with Allied security interests. The term 'escalation control' is relatively new, but the concept itself has always been part and parcel of the flexible response strategy. To stress the close connection with crisis management, one could also speak of 'conflict management'.

Flexibility and diversity of means form the key to both crisis management and conflict management. This can be illustrated by the following imaginary scenario: Soviet ships start to prospect for oil on a part of the Norwegian continental shelf which the Soviet Union claims to be its own. Suppose that non-military means such as diplomatic protests, a UN Security Council resolution or economic sanctions prove unsuccessful in persuading the intruder to withdraw. Dispatching a naval squadron to the scene would then be the obvious next move. The squadron would have to be large enough to discourage any Soviet counter-move. If NATO had no warships available or at least none available in the area, it would be confronted with the dilemma of either acquiescing in the intrusion or going into action in some other area where sufficient means would be available. The first option would only encourage further infringements on Norwegian sovereignty. The second option could mean a dangerous widening of the conflict. If the appropriate means are available and capable of getting to the spot in a short time, the crisis can be settled rapidly and locally without creating excessive tension.

A demonstration of one's resolve often suffices to end the crisis, so that no military force actually needs to be applied. In 1973, for example, Henry Kissinger, then US Secretary of State, managed to dissuade the Soviets from intervening in the Yom Kippur war, simply by putting the US forces on alert.

The efforts to control events do not cease after the outbreak of hostilities. NATO would continuously endeavour to terminate any conflict at the lowest possible level. Paradoxically, in order to terminate the fighting, it might first be necessary to amplify it, if the opponent is not convinced of the Allies' resolve to defend themselves with all available means. Political leaders must then constantly seek a careful balance between the need to demonstrate their resolve on the one hand and the wish to avoid escalation on the other. When nuclear weapons are involved, it is of course all the more important to keep a tight rein on the escalation process.

NATO does not exclude the possibility that, if confronted with an overwhelming armoured thrust by Warsaw Pact forces, it would be the first to cross the nuclear threshold. Such first use would probably be on a limited scale by way of warning, in order to make clear to the aggressor that he has underestimated the risks he is taking. Although it cannot be excluded that the adversary would raise the odds, there is a chance that a nuclear shot across the bows would persuade him to halt the invasion. It is a calculated risk that could restore deterrence.

Without a whole range of means, which enable them carefully to adapt every step to the needs of the moment, the Allies might at a certain point have no option but to escalate more than would otherwise be necessary, with the obvious adverse impact on the further containment of the crisis or conflict.

There is of course no guarantee whatsoever that a process that starts with a few small nuclear exchanges can be contained. The alternative, however, is an all-out nuclear war which would devastate the two superpowers and Europe *alike*. Every effort to control escalation should therefore be made. This does not mean that NATO should in any way envisage waging a protracted nuclear battle in Europe. That would devastate the continent, and the outcome in a military sense could very well not be in NATO's favour. A nuclear exchange cannot and should not in any sense be compared with traditional warfare — although Soviet military strategists tend so to compare it. Any nuclear strike is primarily designed as a political signal, but if it is to perform its political function it should be militarily effective. If the signal in or about the combat area proves insufficient, then it follows from NATO strategy that the signal should be repeated nearer to the Soviet leadership.

Nuclear release procedures

The United States maintains positive control in peace and war over all NATO nuclear weapons except those belonging to the United Kingdom and France. The United States President alone can authorise the use of American nuclear weapons in Europe, following appropriate consultation with the Allies. The United States has transferred nuclear-capable delivery vehicles to the Allies through bilateral 'Programmes of Co-operation'. The warheads for these systems are maintained under the physical control of US custodial detachments until released by the US President. (The Soviet Union has followed a similar policy towards its allies, providing them with delivery vehicles while retaining full control over the warheads.)

Each stockpile of US nuclear weapons in Europe, whether allocated to Allied forces or to US forces themselves, is surrounded by extensive and rigorous security measures. A two-man control system and coded locks ('Permissive Action

Links') preclude any unauthorised arming of a warhead. Warheads recently produced also incorporate a command disabling feature that makes it possible to disable them nonviolently to prevent an attempt at unauthorised use.

The release decision is the absolute prerogative of the highest political authority (the same appears to be true in the Soviet Union). The ultimate decision rests with the American President or the British Prime Minister after substantive consultations — to the extent that circumstances permit — have been conducted with the Allies, notably in the framework of the NATO Defence Planning Committee. Rapid and secure communication systems link national capitals, NATO headquarters and commanders in the field to enable the release procedure — including consultations — to be completed within the time available under the prevailing circumstances. Delegation of release authority to military commanders is out of the question. Because all nuclear weapons are locked with secret coded devices, a 'mad colonel', as portrayed in the film *Dr Strangelove*, would not in fact be able to set off anything.

The French nuclear force is not integrated into NATO planning as the British is, but there too release authority rests in the hands of the highest political authority, namely the President of the Republic.

3
SOVIET STRATEGY

No one doubts that the Soviet population desires peace as earnestly as anyone else. If it were allowed, it might even demonstrate against the war machine forged by its own military, just as Western peace-marchers protest against American armaments. Reality, however, forces one to acknowledge that the individual Soviet citizen is part of a highly militarised system. It is this system we have to deal with. The present chapter therefore focuses on the ideology and military strategy of the Soviet state.

According to Marxism-Leninism, international relations are part of the class struggle. In Stalin's day, war between the capitalist and the socialist camps was considered inevitable. Stalin's successors realised that a war, which in their view was bound to be fought with all available means including nuclear weapons, might jeopardise the achievements of socialism. They therefore introduced the concept of 'peaceful co-existence between states belonging to the opposing social systems'. Peaceful co-existence and its derivative, 'relaxation of international tension', modify the struggle between socialism and capitalism so as to avoid a dangerous and destructive war; they do not however pave the way to reconciliation:

> Peaceful coexistence does not spell an end to the struggle between the two world social systems. The struggle will continue between the proletariat and the bourgeoisie, between world Socialism and Imperialism, up to the complete and final victory of Communism on a world-wide scale.[5]

Although war is no longer considered inevitable, it does remain possible and, should it break out, it must be won

5. Professor F. Ryshenko, 'Peaceful Coexistence and the class struggle', *Pravda*, 22 August 1973, transl. in I. Greig, *They Mean what they Say — a Compilation of Soviet Statements*, Foreign Affairs Research Institute, London, 1981, p. 46.

decisively. In order for victory to be certain, superior forces
are needed. Although Soviet leaders, in declarations directed
at Western public opinion, now emphatically deny that they
are striving for military superiority, they are quite candid in
statements for internal consumption about the fact that their
whole system is geared to this end:

> In its political and social essence a new world war will be a
> decisive armed clash between two opposed world social
> systems. This war will naturally end in victory for the
> progressive communist social-economic system over the
> reactionary capitalist social-economic system, which is
> historically doomed to destruction. The guarantee for such
> an outcome of the war is the real balance between the
> political, economic and military forces of the two systems,
> which has changed in favour of the socialist camp.
> However, victory in a future war will not come by itself. It
> must be thoroughly prepared for and assured.
>
> One of the fundamental questions is the problem of
> assuring quantitative and qualitative military-technical
> superiority over the probable aggressor. This requires the
> possession of an appropriate military-economic base and
> the broad enlistment of the forces of science and technology
> to resolve this problem.[6]

A favourable 'correlation of forces' is not only necessary in
the event of war, but serves also in peace time to create propi-
tious conditions for 'ideological warfare', a term which covers
a diversity of activities ranging from propaganda campaigns
in Western Europe to military support of national liberation

6. V.D. Sokolovskiy, *Soviet Military Strategy*, 3rd edn 1968; transl. by
H. Fast Scott, Macdonald and Janes, London, 1975, p. 209. Sokolovskiy, a
Marshal of the Soviet Union, held from 1952 to 1959 the post of Chief of the
General Staff and First Deputy Minister of Defence (the latter post from
1949). Other prominent members of the Soviet military establishment also
contributed to this work under Sokolovskiy's general direction. *Soviet
Military Strategy* was one of the five books nominated for the 1969 Frunze
Prize, which indicates official approval of the views presented and the
esteem in which the book was held.

movements in the Third World. In the words of Marshal Grechko, the military might of the Soviet Union 'has an enormous progressive influence on the course of world events'.[7]

Attitude towards nuclear and chemical weapons

The Western view that nuclear weapons serve only to deter, since there could only be losers in a nuclear war, is explicitly rejected by Soviet strategists. 'There is' says Major-General Milovidov, 'profound error and harm in the disorienting claims of bourgeois ideologues that there will be no victor in a thermonuclear world war. . . .' The General describes this as the attitude of 'nuclear fatalism'. He considers such views harmful because they 'reject the very possibility of mass productive effort under conditions of war with the employment of nuclear weapons'.[8]

Whereas Western strategic thinking has its origin largely in the civilian academic world, in the Soviet Union these matters are the exclusive domain of the military. This explains why Soviet nuclear strategy bears such a heavy imprint of traditional military thinking. Soviet strategists, while recognising the destructiveness of nuclear weapons, seem to regard them as just another instrument, albeit a very powerful one, which can be used to fight and win a war. The Soviets' belief that they could actually win the Third World War stems also from their view of war as a violent form of class struggle. Victory has by definition always to be on the side of the working class. It is disturbing, however, that this line of thought seems to apply to nuclear war too. The definition of 'nuclear missile warfare' in

7. Marshal A.A. Grechko (Minister of Defence and Politbureau member), *The Soviet Armed Forces — The Dependable Guard of Socialist Achievements*, Moscow, 1971, transl. in 'Selected Soviet Military Writings 1970–1975', *Soviet Military Thought*, no. 11, US Govt. Printing Office, p. 178.

8. Major-General A.S. Milovidov, *The Philosophical Heritage of V.I. Lenin and Problems of Contemporary War*, Voyenizdat, Moscow, 1972, transl. in I. Greig, *They Mean what they Say*, op. cit., pp. 77 and 79.

the *Dictionary of Basic Military Terms*[9] illustrates the Soviet attitude:

> *Raketno-Yadernaya Voyna* (nuclear missile warfare) — Warfare in which the decisive means of attaining victory in battle, in an operation, and in armed conflict as a whole, is the nuclear missile — used without restraint by all services — and above all, the strategic nuclear weapon.
>
> Moreover, final victory, even in nuclear missile warfare, is achieved by the united efforts of all services, using conventional means of armed conflict as well.

Soviet military writings show that the ways of obtaining victory in a nuclear war are being studied in great detail. These include the way to recover faster than the capitalist powers in case the war should prove very destructive, so as to emerge victorious in the end. This explains the great importance the Soviets, as compared with NATO nations, attach to civil defence.

Since chemical weapons are less destructive than nuclear ones, it is no wonder that they too have been fully integrated in the Soviet 'war-fighting' (as opposed to deterrent) strategy. Despite the general revulsion which chemical weapons inspire and the fact that their use — except in retaliation — is forbidden by the 1925 Geneva Protocol, the Soviet Union has acquired a chemical arsenal without parallel. The offensive use of lethal nerve gases or incapacitating agents is foreseen in combination with both conventional and nuclear operations. As is quoted below, 'using means and methods with which the enemy is unfamiliar' is one of the ways to produce a surprise effect. It is to be noted in this connection that NATO relies for deterrence primarily on nuclear weapons, although the United States do have a limited chemical retaliatory capability.

The special function which Soviet strategy accords to *un*conventional weapons, seems to be confirmed by some

9. The *Dictionary of Basic Military Terms* was compiled by the General Staff Academy and published in 1965. Transl. in *Soviet Military Thought*, no. 9, US Govt. Printing Office. A similar definition of '*Vnezapnost*' to that cited on p. 31, below, is given by M.M. Kirian in the *Soviet Military Encyclopedia*, Vœnnœ Izdatel'stvo Ministerstva Oborony SSSR, Moscow, 1976, vol. 2, p. 161.

recent events. In 1979, an epidemic of anthrax broke out near Sverdlovsk, probably caused by an accident at what appears to be a biological warfare research and production facility. The development, production or stockpiling of biological agents for military purposes is prohibited by an international convention of which the Soviet Union is a signatory.

Evidence is also surfacing that the Soviets are using a variety of lethal and incapacitating chemical warfare agents, including nerve gases, against the Mujahidin in Afghanistan. Vietnamese forces operating under Soviet supervision have been using toxins and chemical agents to subdue M'Hong villages in Laos and resistance forces in Cambodia. This implies violation of both the Geneva Protocol and the biological weapon convention. The available evidence is detailed in two reports forwarded by the US Secretary of State to Congress and the United Nations in March and November 1982 respectively.

Until some years ago, Soviet strategy assumed that a war would be nuclear from the outset. Because of their destructive effects, nuclear strikes at the very beginning of a war could determine the outcome of battle. As the first one to strike would probably obtain a decisive advantage, the Soviet Union should see to it that it is the one which does so; this is stressed by Soviet military strategists. In recent years Soviet strategists have paid increased attention to the possibility of an initial conventional phase in a conflict. However, they emphasise that the forces should be ready for escalation to the chemical and/or nuclear level at any time and that it would be militarily advantageous to be the first to do so.

The offensive

Soviet strategy prescribes a lightning offensive with the aim of totally defeating the enemy. Officially, such an offensive would be necessary to defend the 'socialist Fatherland' against the 'imperialist warmongers':

> The imperialists are preparing war against our country, a war of general destruction and mass annihilation of the population, using nuclear weapons. Therefore they must be countered with decisive, active operations of our armed

forces, primarily with crushing nuclear blows by strategic weapons. Only in this way can we curb the imperialistic aggressors, frustrate their criminal plans, and rapidly defeat them. Strategic defence, and then a counter-offensive, under present-day conditions cannot assure the attainment of these decisive war aims.

This does not mean that defence as a forced, temporary type of troop combat operation will not have a place in a future war. Our troops should study and master defence in order to master all forms of military operations. But here we are speaking of operational and tactical defence. *Strategic defence and defensive strategy should be decisively rejected as being extremely dangerous to the country.*[10]

The potentially decisive effects of nuclear strikes reinforce, in the Soviet view, the need for an offensive strategy:

> Nuclear weapons have established even more firmly the role of attack as the decisive form of military action, and have made it necessary to accomplish even defensive tasks by active offensive action.[11]

The offensive should be swift and decisive:

> The basic form of combat operations by our troops will be the attack, since it is of decisive importance in achieving victory over the enemy. *Only a decisive attack conducted at high tempos and to a great depth ensures total victory over the enemy.* The goal of the attack lies in the total defeat of the defending enemy and capture of vital areas of his territory. This goal is achieved by destruction of means of mass destruction and the enemy's main groupings *with nuclear weapons*, the fire of other means, and also the forceful advance to a great depth of tank and motorized rifle troops

10. Sokolovskiy, op. cit., p. 284. Here and in subsequent quotations, the emphasis has been inserted by the present author.

11. Lieutenant-General I.G. Zav'yalov, 'The new weapon and Military Art', *Red Star*, October 1970, transl. in 'Selected Soviet Military Writings 1970–1975', *Soviet Military Thought*, no. 11, US Govt. Printing Office, p. 209.

interworking with aviation and airborne landings, and the bold move to the flanks and rear of the enemy and destruction of him piecemeal.'[12]

One of the key principles of Soviet military thinking, which is to be applied at all levels, is that one should have the advantage of surprise on one's side. The *Dictionary of Basic Military Terms* gives the following definition:

> *Vnezapnost* (surprise) — One of the principles of military art, ensuring success in battle and in operations. Surprise makes it possible to inflict heavy losses upon the enemy in short periods of time, to paralyse his will, and to deprive him of the possibility of offering organised resistance. Surprise is achieved in the following ways: by using various types and methods of combat; *by misleading the enemy as to one's own intentions;* by safeguarding the security of operational plans; by decisive action and skilful manoeuvre; *by unexpected use of nuclear weapons; and by using means and methods with which the enemy is unfamiliar.* Surprise may be tactical, operational or strategic.

The great stress that Soviet strategists lay on obtaining surprise goes back to the German invasion of 22 June 1941, which caught the Red Army wholly off-guard. The Soviets now seem determined to have the initiative in any future war and to wage it on the territory of the enemy. If the imperialists, who are by nature 'predatory', appear to be on the verge of attacking the socialist camp, then Soviet strategy prescribes a *pre-emtive* strike:

> To attain the greatest effectiveness, it is recommended that the nuclear strikes be launched at the start of the fire preparations unexpectedly for the enemy. Pre-emption in launching a nuclear strike is considered to be the decisive condition for the attainment of superiority over him and the seizure and retention of the initiative.[13]

12. Colonel V.Ye. Savkin, *The Basic Principles of Operational Art and Tactics*, Moscow, 1972, transl. in *Soviet Military Thought*, no. 4, US Govt. Printing Office, p. 255. (The obscure phrase 'fire of other means' can be taken to mean, e.g., chemical or merely conventional weapons.)

13. Colonel A.A. Sidorenko (Doctor of Military Science and faculty member of the Frunze Military Academy), *The Offensive*, Moscow, 1970, transl. in *Soviet Military Thought*, no. 1, US Govt. Printing Office, p. 115.

Political decision-making

The ideology of the Soviet Union is clearly expansionist and its military strategy, unlike that of NATO, unmistakably offensive. It is hard to judge to what extent the *political* leaders of the Soviet Union will, in a concrete situation, let themselves be guided by the official body of thought. This is likely to depend in part on the influence the *military* exert on the decision-making process.

A school of Western historians — the revisionists — has tried to show that Soviet foreign policy is fundamentally defensive. One of the theses of this school was that Stalin extended Soviet control over Eastern Europe following the Second World War only in order to provide his country with a protective cordon against renewed aggression from the West. According to the revisionists, the Western fears at that time of further Soviet expansion westwards arose from a misinterpretation of Soviet motives.

Defensive considerations probably did play a part in Stalin's decision to bring Eastern Europe within the Soviet orbit. Whereas Soviet moves in Eastern Europe can still be described as 'defensive expansion', it becomes very hard to see anything defensive about the more recent interventions in Angola, Ethiopia and Afghanistan. It is equally difficult to explain away the momentous Soviet military build-up, which includes naval forces and transport aircraft for power projection at great distances, as merely the reflection of exaggerated security needs.

What can undoubtedly be said of the Soviet leaders is that they are cautious. They have shown themselves quite willing to seize any opportunity which offers itself to expand their influence, but have done so only when there appeared to be no serious risks of a direct confrontation with the West as the result. When, during the 1962 Cuban missile crisis, the risks turned out to be higher than they expected, they backed down. Since then the Soviets have managed significantly to transform the overall military balance, which has encouraged them to be more active in seeking opportunities for expansion, notably in Asia and Africa. Nevertheless Soviet expansionism is still clearly restrained by the overriding concern, often voiced by the late party leader Leonid Brezhnev, to avoid a 'thermonuclear war'. Apropos Brezhnev, and his future successors, Henry Kissinger wrote the following:

> While he boasted of Soviet strength, one had the sense that he was not really all that sure of it. Having grown up in a backward society nearly overrun by Nazi invasion, he seemed to feel in his bones the vulnerability of his system. It is my nightmare that his successors, bred in more tranquil times and accustomed to modern technology and military strength, might be freer of self-doubt; with no such inferiority complex, they may believe their own boasts and, with a military establishment now covering the globe, may prove far more dangerous.[14]

These remarks apply to the future successors of Yuri Andropov, who replaced Brezhnev on the latter's death in November 1982, rather than to Andropov himself. The new leader was born in 1914 and thus clearly belongs to the same generation as Brezhnev. Up to the time of going to press, he has continued in the course of Brezhnev's foreign policy.

(No) first use

One of the difficulties in trying to assess Soviet intentions is in deciding how to reconcile some of the harsher language meant for internal consumption with the more conciliatory tone generally used in speeches and writings aimed at a Western public. The problem is exemplified by Soviet declarations on the no-first-use of nuclear weapons. For a number of years the Soviet Union has been proposing to NATO a mutual pledge not to initiate the use of nuclear weapons. These proposals clearly have the double aim of presenting a peace-loving image and of undermining NATO's strategy of nuclear deterrence. The Alliance cannot afford to make a no-first-use declaration because, if made in earnest, it would restrict the American

14. H. Kissinger, *The White House Years*, Little, Brown and Co., Boston, Mass., 1979.

nuclear guarantee to the case of prior Soviet use. There would then no longer be any counterweight in Europe to Soviet preponderance in conventional armaments.[15]

At the second Special Session of the UN on Disarmament held in New York in June 1982, Andrei Gromyko the Soviet Foreign Minister, read out a formal pledge by President Brezhnev that the Soviet Union would never be the first to use nuclear weapons. This carried previous Soviet policy a step further, in that what had earlier been proposed as part of a mutual agreement was now offered unilaterally. Such a declaration is not, of course, a real guarantee, since the Soviet Union's formidable nuclear capabilities remain unaffected. From an arms control perspective, concrete reductions in the arsenals of both sides deserve priority over verbal declarations which neither side could be really sure of being able to live up to at the critical moment.

The interesting question in the context of this chapter is how the no-first-use pledge relates to the emphasis which Soviet military strategy places on the advantages of being the first to resort to nuclear weapons and on the need to pre-empt their possible use by NATO. There is little evidence that the pledge by Brezhnev — which has been re-iterated by his successor, Andropov — reflected a real change in Soviet military strategy as described in this chapter.

In the present situation it is highly unlikely that the Soviet Union would suddenly initiate a nuclear attack on NATO, but what if for some reason a conflict did break out? The Kremlin leaders would of course prefer to defeat NATO by conventional means, but NATO countries are not likely to resign themselves to such an outcome. And if nuclear weapons are to be used, Soviet strategists reason, their forces should resort to them before NATO does. Tangible evidence that the Soviet Union was discarding the offensive aspects of its strategy and bringing it into line with its declared policy of no-first-use would have a far greater confidence-building effect than any mere verbal declaration made at the UN rostrum.

15. For a more extensive discussion of no-first-use from a European point of view, see K. Kaiser, G. Leber, A. Mertes and F.-J. Schulze, 'Nuclear Weapons and the Preservation of Peace', *Foreign Affairs*, Summer 1982.

Theatre warfare

Soviet forces are geared to a massive armoured thrust across the German plains. The way for the invading ground forces might be cleared by means of nuclear and/or chemical strikes:

> The primary method of attack will be the launching of nuclear strikes and the swift advance of tank and motorised rifle *podrazdeleniye* [units of battalion size and smaller] into the depth of the enemy's defence through the breaches formed by nuclear weapons.[16]

It is also possible that hostilities would be initiated with conventional forces only — the nuclear and chemical weapons being held back, but ready for engagement as soon as NATO gives the impression that it might be about to go nuclear itself.

In both its conventional and nuclear phase, 'the primary objective of armed combat in the theatres will be the nuclear weapons of the enemy'.[17] NATO can therefore expect its Theatre Nuclear Forces to be the target of conventional attack (e.g. air raids, airborne assaults and artillery fire), chemical strikes and, above all, nuclear strikes:

> The following requirements are made of the combating of enemy tactical means of nuclear attack: continuity of its conduct, immediate destruction of nuclear means as they are discovered, and *pre-emption in the launching of nuclear strikes, that is, destruction of enemy nuclear means before they can be put into action* . . .
>
> On the whole, it should be said that combating enemy means of nuclear attack in combined arms combat has now become the basic content of combat actions and has become a function of all commanders without exception.[18]

Consequently, for NATO the survivability of its TNF is a matter of constant concern.

Warsaw Pact forces are far better equipped and trained to operate in a radioactive or toxic environment than are their

16. Sidorenko, op. cit., p. 62.
17. Sokolovskiy, op. cit., p. 291.
18. Sidorenko, op. cit., pp. 134–6.

NATO counterparts. For example, all new tanks and armoured personnel carriers are equipped with air filters, and are pressurised so as to protect the crews against radiation and gases. For the speedy decontamination of large quantities of tanks and vehicles, special sprinkler aircraft and trucks are available. Such extensive measures are not only meant to protect the troops against enemy nuclear or chemical strikes, but even more to enable them to exploit *their own* strikes rapidly. Chemical weapons provide the Soviets with great flexibility in this respect, since they can choose between more and less persistent agents. Non-persistent agents can be dropped to deny NATO the use of features like bridges or airfields, which Warsaw Pact forces will want to use themselves once they have reached them. The gases will kill personnel, but after a while the area becomes accessible again. Buildings and infrastructure remain intact.

The presence of nuclear weapons on the NATO side places constraints on offensive operations by Warsaw Pact ground forces (as set out on p. 20). If they are not to offer easy targets, they must avoid the heavy troop concentrations in large assembly areas, which traditionally precede an attack, and need to remain fairly dispersed. The Soviets have developed new tactics to escape possible nuclear counter-blows by NATO without sacrificing the pace of the offensive: their troops would be concentrated very rapidly and close to enemy lines, and contact with the enemy would be sought as soon as possible with the aim of infiltrating his defence positions. Instead of attempting large breakthroughs at division level, a whole series of smaller regiment-level penetrations would be sought. The speed of the attack and the ensuing intermingling of troops would make it almost impossible for NATO to use its nuclear weapons, because of the risk to which this would expose its own troops. (The so called 'neutron bomb', which can be used nearer to friendly troops than present-day nuclear weapons, is meant as an answer to the new Soviet tactics, as is shown on p. 82)

What Soviet reaction can be expected if NATO, unable to withstand a conventional onslaught, fired a nuclear shot across the bows? It has often been predicted that the Soviets would then react on a massive scale with their much larger,

Above: the scene immediately after the SALT II Treaty was signed by Presidents Carter and Brezhnev in Vienna on 18 June 1979. The Treaty remains of fundamental importance even though it was never ratified. *Below:* the INF negotiators, Paul Nitze and Yuli Kvitsinskiy, meeting in Geneva.

Above: Yuri Andropov, Brezhnev's successor as General Secretary of the CPSU. The similarities with the Brezhnev era are more striking than the differences. *Below:* the Prague summit of 4–5 January 1983, which initiated a new peace offensive: Andropov and his East European colleagues.

Right: a Soviet 'Scud' missile being made ready for launching. The range is 300 km. *Below:* artist's impression of the SS-20, also being made ready.

Above: the new Soviet 'Backfire' bomber, carrying an AS-4 'Kitchen' cruise missile (range 450 km.). Although intended primarily for use against Europe, the 'Backfire' also has a certain intercontinental capability. *Below:* the first generation of Soviet Eurostrategic systems: two 'Badger' bombers, each carrying an AS-2 'Kipper' cruise missile with a range of 180 km.

Above: the 'blue' grey area: a Soviet cruise missile submarine of the *Juliett* class. *Below:* a US ground-launched cruise missile (GLCM) of the type to be deployed in five European countries.

The 'Pershing' II. The Soviets are eager to prevent its deployment in West Germany, but if they succeed in this aim, they will have to pay the price in SS-20s.

It would be difficult for Western aircraft to get through the dense network of Soviet air defence missiles such as SA-2 'Guidelines' (*above*). *Below:* the USS *Forrestal*, one of the twelve US aircraft-carriers. Their ability to project power ashore depends on their ability to secure control of the seas first and to fend off Soviet land-based naval bombers.

Cartoon by Hans Behrendt © *Het Parool*, Amsterdam.

inaccurate warheads. In other words, efforts by NATO to control escalation and keep destruction to a minimum are bound to fail, because the Soviets would not play the game by our rules.

There is both a military and a political dimension to this question. To start with the military dimension, it is a fact that the first generations of Soviet theatre missiles had larger warheads than those of NATO to compensate for their lack of accuracy. However, it does not follow that Soviet strategy advocates mass destruction in the theatre; on the contrary, in keeping with its line of traditional military thinking, it advocates concentrating all effort on destroying the opposing forces. Counter-city strikes within the theatre are explicitly rejected in Soviet writings because they would distract attention from the military defeat of the enemy, hamper the advance of attacking units, and remove infrastructure and supplies needed for their own troops. The older tactical missiles are now all being replaced by sophisticated and highly accurate new ones, equipped with lower-yield warheads. Thus Soviet ability to launch discriminate and selective strikes both in the combat area and in the enemy rear is constantly increasing.

As for the political dimension of the matter, a massive and indiscriminate response to a shot across the bows would imply that the Kremlin leaders had abandoned their traditional prudence and decided to go it all the way. So long as they have not reached this stage, which it seems they would only be likely to do in the most extreme circumstances, the idea that they would to some extent match Western restraint remains plausible. Bearing in mind the reluctance Soviet leaders have shown to take heavy risks, there is a chance that a shot across the bows would persuade them that they had miscalculated the risks involved, thus inducing them to suspend their attack. However, there is obviously no certain way that the reactions of either side in such hypothetical circumstances can be predicted.

4

THE MILITARY BALANCE

'The correlation of forces between the two blocs has shifted to the advantage of the socialist camp,' the late Soviet Prime Minister, Alexei Kosygin, wrote in *Communist* in May 1980. It is a fact that the Soviet Union has gradually managed to increase its weight in world politics. In the wake of the Second World War, it made substantial territorial gains at the expense of neighbouring countries and installed pro-Soviet regimes in Eastern Europe. When their expansion in Europe came to a halt after the failure to coerce the Western powers into leaving West Berlin, the Soviets switched their attention to the Third World. Although they suffered some setbacks there, they have nevertheless succeeded in wringing naval and air facilities from a string of client states.

The emergence of the Soviet Union as a superpower equal to the United States rests primarily on its military might. Its political and economic systems continue to be plagued by problems, which have arisen in particularly acute form in Poland. In the military field a relentless build-up, sustained over two decades, has gradually changed the overall military balance. This does not imply that the Warsaw Pact has acquired absolute military superiority; in some areas it has done so, in others not. But it does mean that most force ratios have significantly changed and continue to change as the East outbuilds the West in many major weapon categories. In addition, the qualitative edge on which the West traditionally relied to offset some of its quantitative deficiencies has been whittled down.

To sustain its massive build-up, the Soviet Union has been devoting, since the mid-1960s, an average of around 2.5 times more of its Gross National Product (GNP) to military purposes than the United States or NATO countries.[19] The

19. The Soviet Union devoted 11–13 per cent of its GNP to military purposes between 1965 and 1978 and 12–14 per cent in 1979 and 1980 (CIA estimates). The US figure increased from 5.1 per cent in 1979 to 5.9 per cent in 1981; the NATO average from 4.2 to 4.8 per cent (according to NATO computations released in December 1982).

annual increase of Soviet defence expenditure has averaged about 4 per cent in real terms and shows few signs of levelling off, despite slowing economic growth rates (see Chart 4). US real-term defence spending actually decreased throughout most of the 1970s. In 1977, NATO pledged itself to increase its defence spending by 3 per cent in real terms every year, a target the United States generally managed to meet and is now even surpassing, but which other member-countries have found difficult to meet.

The aggregate NATO GNP is of course much higher than that of the Warsaw Pact. However, because of lower wages, the Pact devotes a much larger share of its military expenditure to capital investment. Furthermore, greater standardisation of equipment enables it to produce weapons more cost-effectively.

The sections which follow review first, briefly, the conventional and strategic balance and then, in greater detail, the tactical nuclear balance.

There are many ways to assess the balance. The simplest is the 'bean count': a straightforward comparison of numbers of aircraft, tanks etc. Such comparisons can be instructive, but do not provide the full picture. A more sophisticated assessment would, for instance, examine how the offensive airpower of one side would interact with the air defences of the other side; how tanks would interact with the opposing anti-tank capability, and so on.

Of the many factors that ought to be taken into account in force comparisons the most basic is probably the differences in mission. Warsaw Pact forces in Central Europe are organised, equipped and trained for a fast drive through the German plains towards the North Sea. NATO forces are geared to prevent such a move. Clearly forces with such different missions have different requirements. NATO need not match the Warsaw Pact tank for tank, man for man, provided that it has adequate overall defensive power.

Assessments of the balance depend on the scenario, in particular the degree of surprise achieved by the attacker. Normally the attacker has the advantage of having started war preparations earlier than the defender. The longer he manages to conceal his preparations, the greater his advantage. The time factor is crucial, because both sides rely heavily on the mobilisation of reservists and have to move up reinforcements to the combat area.

The attacker also has the advantage of being the one to determine where and when he will concentrate his main effort. The defender, on the other hand, will have to spread his forces evenly along all the possible avenues of attack.

Another important factor influencing the balance is geography. The Warsaw Pact countries form one contiguous land mass, which offers the advantage of shorter and interior lines of communication. NATO is more fragmented, and its European members are heavily dependent for their defence on reinforcements that have to cross an ocean 6,000 km. wide. While geography favours Warsaw Pact ground and air forces over those of NATO, it places constraints on Warsaw Pact naval forces, which dispose of only few ice-free harbours and can only reach the high seas through so-called 'choke points' (e.g. the Bosphorus and the Dardanelles and the straits between Denmark and Southern Sweden).

There are of course many other factors besides the military which weigh in the balance: the economic, the political — and, not least, the human factor, which plays a role at all levels.

The conventional balance

Warsaw Pact ground forces traditionally enjoy a great numerical advantage, especially in Europe. This advantage can be illustrated in different ways. On a world-wide basis the Warsaw Pact has 60,000 main battle tanks as against 22,670 for NATO. In Europe the ratio is 42,500[20] as against 13,000.[21] Furthermore, Eastern tank production rates surpass those in the West. On average, NATO tanks are probably still better,

20. Excluding Soviet strategic reserves in the Moscow, Ural and Volga Military Districts.

21. The figures given in this and the previous sentences refer to countries participating in NATO's integrated military structure only. French tank holdings are 1,140, according to *The Military Balance 1982–1983*. Spanish figures are not yet included.

but this qualitative edge is dwindling with the introduction on a large scale of the new Soviet T-72 and T-80 tanks, which are considered to be on a par with recent NATO models. Also, contrary to what one might expect, Warsaw Pact forces maintain larger numbers of anti-tank weapons (see Chart 3).

NATO has always heavily depended on its air forces to blunt an attack and slow down enemy reinforcements. Although outnumbered, NATO aircraft still enjoy a clear qualitative advantage.

Warsaw Pact air forces used to be primarily geared to air defence. This changed in the course of the 1970s through the introduction of modern fighter-bombers and bombers capable of conducting interdiction and air superiority strikes deep into NATO territory, including the aerial and maritime ports of entry for overseas reinforcements. At the same time the Warsaw Pact modernized its air defences, which are far more extensive than NATO's. The large numbers of interceptor aircraft and surface-to-air missiles (SAMs) would make it difficult for NATO aircraft to penetrate into enemy territory.

Twenty years ago Western naval forces enjoyed uncontested maritime supremacy. The Soviet Navy concentrated on the protection of the homeland and adjacent waters. From the coastal defence force it then was, the Soviet Navy has been transformed into an ocean-going force capable of projecting power at great distances from its homeland in a manner that used to be reserved to such traditional naval powers as the United States and Great Britain.

Western naval forces are on the whole still considered more capable than the Eastern. The Warsaw Pact has slightly more ships, but NATO has a substantially larger aggregate tonnage, which is a better indicator of naval capability. Such comparisons in absolute terms are only of limited comfort, because the sea is much more important to NATO. Western Europe is heavily dependent on raw materials from the Third World, and in wartime a constant stream of US reinforcements and supplies would be crossing the Atlantic. It requires a great deal more ships to keep vital sea lanes open than to interrupt them. If one bears in mind the tonnage sunk by the relatively small German submarine fleet in the First and Second World

Wars it is easy to imagine what the 388 Warsaw Pact sub-marines[22] could do to the West's supply lines in the 1980s.

The strategic nuclear balance

The strategic nuclear arsenals of the two superpowers can be described as roughly equivalent, with a trend towards Soviet superiority. The adverse trend will to some extent be reversed in the second half of the 1980s, when deployments of new American systems, now being developed, will begin. The United States have set themselves the aim of maintaining 'essential equivalence', a concept which makes allowance for dissimilarities in the two strategic arsenals. For instance, the Soviets have a lead in the total number of launchers as well as in the aggregate throw-weight and megatonnage. The United States is still ahead in the number of warheads.

In the 1950s and early 1960s the United States enjoyed over-whelming strategic superiority. By the early 1970s, the Soviet Union had caught up with the United States in numbers of launchers. Americans expected the Soviet effort to level off once parity had been achieved, and as a consequence the number of US launchers was not increased beyond the 1967 level, as Chart 2 indicates. The only major programme to be implemented in the 1970s consisted of fitting existing missiles with MIRVs (Multiple Independently-targetable Re-entry Vehicles — the 're-entry vehicles' are the several warheads which a missile discharges when re-entering the atmosphere). New programmes like the 'Trident' submarine and the M-X ICBM were slowed down. The B–1 bomber project was (temporarily) cancelled.

These signs of unilateral restraint had no effect on the momentum of the Soviet strategic build-up. The Soviets deployed *inter alia* an entire new generation — the fourth — of ICBMs, and in the late 1970s started an extensive MIRV programme of their own. This elicited this remark from the then US Secretary of Defense Harold Brown: 'We have found that when we build weapons, they build; when we stop, they nevertheless continue to build.'[23]

22. USSR: 273 operational and 107 in reserve. NSWP: 8. 'Military Balance 1982–83'.
23. Hearing on the SALT II treaty before the US Senate Committee on Foreign Relations; July 1979, US Govt. Printing Office, part 1, p. 111.

One source of concern is the counter-force potential of two of the new Soviet ICBMs: the SS–18, a behemoth containing ten MIRVs, and the SS–19 with its six MIRVs. These missiles combine the traditional large size of Soviet warheads with unprecedented accuracy, a combination well suited for destroying highly protected or 'hardened' targets (i.e. those dug in and/or protected by concrete to resist explosions) such as underground ICBM silos. Theoretically the (approximately) 4,800 warheads of the 308 SS–18s and 310 SS–19s could eliminate in one surprise stroke most US launcher silos. By way of comparison, the 550 'Minuteman' III ICBMs, the newest US ICBM and the only one with a certain capability against hardened targets, comprise a total of 1,650 warheads (three MIRVs each). This illustrates the extent of the Soviet lead in 'time-urgent hard target kill capability', i.e. the capability to hit targets that can be moved or launched rapidly. (Current SLBMs have only a very limited capability against hard targets; bombers are not suited for a surprise attack because of their long flight time.) Introduction of the M-X by the United States would reduce, but not undo, the Soviet lead in counter-silo capability.

Vulnerability of the ICBM leg of the strategic triad may not be equated to vulnerability of the whole triad. The Soviets may be nearing the point of a theoretical first strike capability against American ICBMs, but SLBMs are still virtually invulnerable, and those bombers which are on alert have a good chance of taking off before any ballistic missile hits their base.

For the sake of completeness, the British strategic forces and in a sense also those of France should be included with those of the United States in the NATO total. However, this makes little difference to the overall balance because these forces are comparatively small.

In summary, although it once trailed far behind, the Soviet Union has managed to catch up with the United States in the strategic field. Since the early 1970s the situation has generally been described as one of approximate parity. The SALT agreements (see pp. 66 ff.) tried to freeze this situation, but in fact did not halt the shift in the balance. While in the early 1970s one could still have spoken of 'parity plus' in favour of the United States, today 'parity minus' would be more apt.

The disappearance of US strategic superiority has altered the whole context of East-West relations and, more specifically, it has increased the importance of the lower rungs of the escalation ladder. The former West German Chancellor, Helmut Schmidt, drew attention to this point as early as 1977:

> 'SALT codifies the nuclear strategic balance between the Soviet Union and the United States. To put it another way: SALT neutralises their strategic nuclear capabilities. In Europe this magnifies the significance of the disparities between East and West in nuclear tactical and conventional weapons.'[24]

The theatre nuclear balance: problems of analysis

The tactical/theatre nuclear balance is the most difficult to assess. The great diversity of systems involved is one reason for this. Another is that TNF form the transition between conventional and strategic forces and cannot therefore easily be dissociated from either of these other types of forces. Already in the first chapter we have pointed out that longer-range theatre systems and strategic systems can sometimes be used interchangeably, as is illustrated by the fact that some Soviet ICBMs (SS–11s) are believed to be targeted on Europe. Shorter-range TNF, on the other hand, are meant, in military terms, to support conventional operations. The ability of conventional forces to sustain tactical nuclear strikes and to pursue operations in a nuclear environment is crucial to any analysis of the theatre nuclear balance. The high losses that can be expected from any tactical nuclear exchange are one more reason for the Warsaw Pact to maintain such large forces.

The difficulties encountered in any separate assessment of the TNF balance are compounded by the existence of *dual-capable* systems; these are systems that can be used in both a conventional and a nuclear role, such as some types of aircraft. Most dual-capable systems would be engaged in an initial phase of a conflict that was exclusively conventional,

24. Alastair Buchan Memorial lecture, 28 October 1977.

and losses incurred would weaken the nuclear capability available for any later phase.

Figures for combat aircraft and other dual-capable systems often vary because they are computed on the basis of different definitions. The difficulty is that if a certain type of aircraft is technically dual-capable, it does not necessarily follow that all units are actually assigned a nuclear role and that crews have been trained accordingly. Some squadrons/regiments may have a dual role, others only a conventional one. In general, the longer the range of an aircraft and the heavier the payload it can carry, the greater the likelihood that it has a nuclear role. Technically, the difference between a purely conventional aircraft and one that can also perform nuclear missions is slight; often it is only a matter of some extra wiring. Thus, an arms control agreement that was only designed to limit aircraft with a nuclear role, leaving the rest unconstrained, could easily be circumvented. For arms control purposes the total inventory is the more relevant figure.

As with conventional forces, TNF can be compared either on a world-wide basis or theatre by theatre. The latter approach is more common, but it involves some difficulties, such as how to define the boundaries of the theatre and to what extent reinforcement capabilities should be taken into account.

In the following sections, the nuclear systems of NATO and Warsaw Pact affecting the balance in land theatres are reviewed. The maritime balance under nuclear circumstances will be assessed in a subsequent section.

Warsaw Pact nuclear forces affecting the balance in land theatres

In the mid 1960s the Soviet Union maintained some 700 SS–4 and SS–5 missiles, most of them aimed at Europe. Together with the Soviet ICBMs, these missiles form the 'Strategic Rocket Forces', but Western assessments count them as LRTNF (longer-range INF in the new terminology). In 1977 a replacement appeared for the SS–4 and SS–5: the SS–20, with its substantially improved performance characteristics. Its range is 4,400–5,000 km. as compared to 1,900 and 4,100 km. for the SS–4 and SS–5 respectively. Whereas the SS–4 and SS–5 stand in fixed, unprotected sites, the SS–20 is mobile and so, unlike its predecessors, is almost invulnerable.

. The SS–4 and SS–5 can only be launched after their liquid fuel has been added, an elaborate and time-consuming procedure providing ample warning. The SS–20 uses a solid propellant and can therefore be launched without delay. This makes it a suitable instrument with which to initiate a surprise attack. Another significant difference is that, whereas the SS–4 and SS–5 are each fitted with one warhead of megaton size, the SS–20 has three MIRVs with smaller yield (in the order of 150 kilotons) and much greater accuracy. This gives the Soviet Union a theatre-wide counter-force capability which it previously lacked.

No less than 315 SS–20 launchers were deployed by mid–1982,[25] totalling 945 warheads. Of these, more than 70 per cent are within range of NATO Europe. In addition, the SS–20 has a refire capability. By mid–1982 the number of SS–4s had gone down to 265 and of SS–5s to fifteen. On 16 March 1982, President Brezhnev had announced a partial stop of SS–20 deployments (see p. 107), but deployments have been continuing since that date without interruption throughout the Soviet Union. The end of the whole SS–20 programme is still not in sight.

Attention has focused on Soviet LRTNF modernisation, but all the shorter-range missiles are being replaced too. The 900-km. 'Scaleboard' missile, assigned at 'front' level, is beginning to be replaced by the SS–22, which has a similar range. The 'Frog', a rocket with a range of up to 70 km., is being replaced by the more capable SS–21, ranging about 120 km. and comparable to the Western 'Lance'. Every Warsaw Pact division is equipped with four 'Frog' launchers, making a total of about 885 (for further details about the figures see the tables on pp. 120–3). It seems likely that similar numbers of SS–21s will ultimately be deployed. The 500 km. SS–23 missile has been developed to replace the 300 km.

25. July figures. By March 1983, the number of SS–20 launchers had been increased to 351, of which 243 are targeted on NATO Europe and 108 on China and Japan; SS–4 and SS–5 launchers had by then been decreased to about 230 and 15 respectively.

'Scud', of which about twelve are assigned to every Warsaw Pact army (a total of some 683 launchers). All these 'operational and tactical missiles', as the Soviets describe them, can be fitted with either a nuclear, chemical or conventional warhead. 'Scuds' and 'Frogs' have also been provided to non-Soviet Warsaw Pact forces. The warheads, however, remain in Soviet custody.

For a long time only NATO possessed dual-capable artillery. In the past few years, however, the Soviet Union has adapted artillery pieces and even mortars to fire nuclear projectiles, thus filling the last gap in its capabilities.

Soviet 'Long-Range Aviation' consists — in addition to intercontinental bombers — of a large fleet of continental bombers ('Badgers' and 'Blinders'). A successor to these now obsolescent aircraft appeared in 1974: the 'Backfire', a high-performance supersonic bomber. The 'Backfire' is primarily designed for strike missions in the theatres on the periphery of the Soviet Union — Europe and the Far East — but with in-flight refuelling or Arctic staging, it can reach the United States too. For this reason it has been discussed in the context of strategic arms control. Some 100 'Backfires' have been introduced into Long-Range Aviation and about eighty into 'Naval Aviation', as will be seen in the maritime section. Production is continuing at the rate of thirty units a year. The number of 'Badgers' and 'Blinders' in a ground-attack role has declined to about 435.

All Soviet bombers can carry nuclear or conventional free-fall bombs or cruise missiles, notably the AS–3, AS–4, AS–5 and AS–6. These air-launched cruise missiles (ALCMs) can be either nuclear or conventionally armed. They have ranges up to 600 km. and, because of their supersonic speed, are very difficult to intercept. The advantage of equipping bombers with ALCMs is that they are thus enabled to strike at their target, while remaining out of reach of the surrounding air defences.

Some of the Soviet ALCMs carried by Backfires and other bombers have been in service for quite some time. They are faster than the ALCMs with which the United States is now equipping its B–52s, but can in no way compete in range or accuracy with the new generation of American cruise missiles whose technology is much more sophisticated. Cruise missile technology is however not standing still in the Soviet Union either, and new longer-range types are being developed there too.

Soviet 'Frontal Aviation' (the equivalent of tactical air forces in the West) has been re-equipped over the past ten years with large numbers of new dual-capable fighter-bombers with substantially increased ranges, payloads and speeds. The most potent of these are the later models 'Fitter' and 'Flogger' and above all the 'Fencer'. The 'Fencer' is a heavy fighter-bomber with a comparatively extensive combat radius, which puts much of Western Europe within its reach from home bases in the Soviet Union. Its target coverage is being further increased by forward deployment to bases in East Germany, Poland and Hungary. Some 550 'Fencers' are operational. Deployments are continuing.

Finally, some Soviet sea-based systems that could influence events in land theatres should be mentioned. In 1976, six older diesel-powered 'Golf' II submarines, each armed with three 1,400-km. SS–N–5 SLBMs, which used to patrol off the coasts of the United States, were assigned to the Baltic Fleet as a supplement to existing theatre capabilities (these submarines have not been counted under SALT). The Soviet Navy also has a wide array of surface ships and submarines that are specifically designed to carry cruise missiles. Most of these cruise missiles have a nuclear and conventional anti-ship role (see maritime section). But some of them, like the SS–N–3, which has a range of up to 450 km., can also be used for nuclear strikes against targets along the shore. The SS–N–3 is now being replaced by the 550-km. range SS–N–12, and an even newer model is being introduced: the SS–N–19, which has a range of 450 km. Since a large part of the big cities and centres of industrial activity in North America and Western Europe are concentrated in the coastal regions, many vital targets are within range of Soviet SLCMs.

NATO nuclear forces affecting the balance in land theatres

NATO has no equivalent at present to the Soviet LRTNF (longer-range INF) missile force. It did once maintain 'Thor' and 'Jupiter' LRTNF missiles in the United Kingdom, Italy and Turkey, but these were withdrawn between 1963 and 1965. Now the only land-based missiles in Western Europe that can reach the Soviet Union are eighteen *Missiles Sol-Sol Balistiques Stratégiques* (SSBS) of the French strategic forces, which are not assigned to NATO.

The NATO countries participating in the integrated military structure do have 180 medium-range TNF (shorter-range INF) 'Pershing' I missiles. Of these, 108 are manned by US troops and seventy-two by German troops. They have a range of about 750 km. All the warheads are under US control.

Confronted with a growing LRTNF imbalance, NATO decided in December 1979 to deploy in Europe 464 US ground-launched cruise missiles (GLCMs)(range 2,500 km.) and to replace the 108 US 'Pershings' by a successor model, the 'Pershing' II, with a longer range (1,800 km.). Unless an arms control agreement can be reached, deployment of these new systems will start in December 1983 (see Chapter 8).

NATO army corps, especially those in Central Europe, have at their disposal a total of about 100 shorter-range 'Lance' missiles (range 120 km.). In addition, part of their artillery, some 1,000 pieces, is dual-capable.

The bulk of NATO's theatre nuclear capability consists of dual-capable aircraft. Of these only a comparatively small number of medium bombers have sufficient combat radius to strike targets in the Soviet Union itself: 164 US F–111s stationed in Europe and forty-eight ageing British 'Vulcans' which are to be replaced by 'Tornado' fighter-bombers. The latter have a much shorter range. French strategic forces have thirty-seven 'Mirage' IV bombers — but again these are not assigned to NATO. NATO has various types of dual-capable fighter-bombers, including sizeable numbers of 'Starfighters' and 'Phantoms'. Their replacement by 'Tornados' and F–16s will help preserve NATO's technological edge in terms of air forces.

Air power on NATO's flanks could be strengthened by varying numbers of US aircraft-carriers. Although carrier air wings are likely to operate primarily in a conventional mode, they do include a number of technically dual-capable attack aircraft, generally ten A–6 'Intruders' and twenty-four A–7

'Corsairs'. It cannot be taken for granted that in a global conflict carriers would be available for operations against land targets. They are likely to be very much absorbed by the contest for sea control. Moreover, as soon as a carrier attempted to approach the European coast, it would be exposed to 'Backfires' and other Soviet land-based naval aircraft.

France has two carriers, whose air wings each include twelve dual-capable attack aircraft.

The qualitative edge of NATO aircraft is largely offset by the greater size of the Warsaw Pact's air forces and its much more extensive air defence network. Warsaw Pact surface-to-air missiles (SAM) and fighter-interceptors markedly reduce the probability that NATO strike aircraft — land-based or sea-based — would reach their targets.

Differences between American and Soviet cruise missile technology were described in the previous section. The United States now has several kinds of cruise missile in production. Only GLCMs will affect the theatre nuclear balance. ALCMs will be mounted on strategic bombers. Most sea-launched cruise missiles (SLCMs) are designed to supplement the Navy's anti-ship capabilities. A nuclear land-attack version of the 'Tomahawk' SLCM to be placed on submarines is planned as a strategic reserve.

The United States has placed a certain number of strategic submarines fitted with 'Poseidon' SLBMs at the disposal of SACEUR. Despite their assignment to a regional commander, these systems remain inherently strategic and are counted in SALT.

Two NATO members have similar systems of their own: Great Britain has four submarines equipped with US-made 'Polaris' SLBMs. They are assigned to SACEUR, but at the same time serve as the ultimate national strategic deterrent. France has five wholly French-manufactured ballistic missile submarines in her strategic forces.

Qualitative and quantitative shifts in the balance

The nuclear balance in the European theatre has shifted over the past decade in quantitative terms, and even more so in qualitative terms. The Soviet Union modernised its TNF at a faster pace than NATO, introducing a far greater number of new systems. Modernisation of longer-range TNF got underway first — in the mid-1970s — and accentuated the range asymmetries between NATO and the Warsaw Pact. Modernisation of Warsaw Pact shorter-range TNF is only beginning.

One of the most significant developments is the shift in the relative vulnerability of the two sides. This has been brought about by the major improvements in terms of range, survivability and ability to penetrate of the new Soviet systems. A case in point is the SS–20, which has a substantially increased range and much greater pre-launch survivability than its predecessors. The SS–4s and SS–5s, as we have seen, were deployed in easily observable fixed sites and could only be launched after cumbrous fuelling procedures, during which the site was vulnerable to counter-attack. The SS–20, besides being mobile and therefore much more difficult to detect, can be launched without delay, which deprives NATO of prior warning and the possibility of taking countermeasures. Conversely, the greater range and accuracy of the SS–20 and the greater speed with which it can be launched diminish the pre-launch survivability of Allied TNF. NATO aircraft could be caught by surprise on the ground and French strategic missiles destroyed in their silos.

NATO's sea-based aircraft have grown more vulnerable too. Because of the increased sophistication of Soviet sea-launched and air-launched cruise missiles, one has to reckon with the possibility that carriers would be disabled before approaching sufficiently close to the continent to launch their aircraft.

The diminished pre-launch survivability of NATO aircraft is paralleled by their reduced ability to get through the increasingly dense air defences of the Warsaw Pact. Penetrating into the Soviet heartland itself, shielded as it is by 10,000 SAM launchers and 2,600 interceptors, would be particularly hazardous. NATO's relatively few theatre-wide bombers (mainly F–111s) would face a very difficult task. The density of the Warsaw Pact's air defences has additional implications, in that the bulk of NATO's theatre strike potential consists of aircraft. No such problem confronts the Soviet Union, because a much larger part of its arsenal consists of ballistic missiles, which — unlike aircraft — have a 100 per cent penetration probability.

The vulnerability of Western Europe has also increased as a result of the introduction into the Soviet air force of new high-performance strike aircraft ('Backfire', 'Fencer' etc.). NATO's air defences have not kept pace with the development of Soviet offensive air power.

In numerical terms, NATO's TNF are inferior to the Warsaw Pact in all categories except dual-capable artillery, as can be seen from the tables on pp. 120–3. The most striking imbalance is in the field of long-range TNF (longer-range INF). The Soviet Union has a virtual monopoly in land-based missiles and one and a half times as many theatre bombers with a land-attack mission.[26] Even if the British and French strategic SLBMs were counted against Soviet theatre missiles — although the two cannot really be compared — the Soviet Union would still retain an enormous advantage in terms of both launchers and warheads on launchers.

The Warsaw Pact has over four times as many medium-range TNF missiles (shorter-range INF) as NATO (compare the numbers of 'Scaleboards' and 'Scuds' with the number of 'Pershings'). Furthermore, it has nearly twice as many land-based fighter-bombers with a nuclear role if one compares world-wide capabilities, and more than twice as many if one considers Europe only.[27] NATO carrier-based aircraft can be included in the comparisons, but then Soviet Naval Aviation has to be brought in too, and force ratios would hardly be affected.

With regard to short-range TNF, the situation is more balanced. NATO has more dual-capable tube artillery and a slight overall numerical advantage. The Warsaw Pact, however, has more rockets and missiles which, because of their greater range compared to artillery, more than compensate for NATO's slight overall numerical advantage.

26. If the 'Fencer' is counted as a bomber, the Soviet Union would have twice as many bombers.

27. If the 'Fencer' is counted as a bomber, the Warsaw Pact fighter-bomber advantage would be slightly less: one and a half on a worldwide basis and somewhat above one and a half in Europe.

The above comparisons focus on delivery vehicles (missile launchers and aircraft). Much less is known about the warheads available to both sides. The United States have about 6,000 warheads in Europe. In so far as delivery vehicles are a guide to the number of warheads, the Soviet Union can be presumed to have more. On the SS–20s alone, 1053 warheads have been deployed.[28]

The maritime balance

The respective naval forces of NATO and the Warsaw Pact have very different missions. NATO's would try to establish control over the seas and keep vital supply routes open. Warsaw Pact fleets would attempt to interdict Western sea lines of communication and prevent US aircraft-carriers from interfering with the land battle.

US aircraft-carriers are the mainstay of the Western naval forces. Twelve are operational, with 408 attack aircraft aboard as well as considerable numbers of air defence and anti-submarine aircraft. Sea control would be the first mission of the carriers. To this end their aircraft would attack enemy ships within a wide perimeter. Another mission of the carriers is to project power ashore, for example through air strikes against Soviet naval and air bases.

Thus far the Soviet Union has not really tried to match the US carrier force. At present it has only three smaller carriers; however, a full-size carrier is expected late in the 1980s. The Soviet answer to Western superiority in major surface combatants and shipboard aircraft has been the cruise missile. As early as the 1950s the Soviet Union started fitting submarines with conventional and nuclear anti-ship cruise missiles. At present it has about seventy submarines specially designed to carry such cruise missiles, as well as various types of surface ships. The first of an entirely new class of cruise missile submarines, called the *Oscar* class, was introduced in 1981. It carries twenty-four SS–N–19 cruise missiles with a range of 450 km.

To keep Western carriers and other surface ships at a

28. See footnote 25, above.

distance, the Soviet Union has built up a powerful land-based naval air force, comprising strike bombers — some 270 'Badgers', forty 'Blinders' and eighty 'Backfires' — as well as various other types of aircraft. The bombers are equipped with conventional or nuclear cruise missiles, which can hit a warship at a distance of several hundred kilometres.[29] US aircraft-carriers are surrounded by extensive defences, including sophisticated interceptor aircraft and escort ships. One nevertheless wonders how long they could fend off co-ordinated 'saturation attacks' by SLCMs, reinforced by ALCMs, once the ships had come within range of land-based 'Backfires'. (Introduction of the 'Backfire', which has a combat radius of about 4,200 km., greatly extended the reach of the Soviet Navy's air arm.) Whether carriers could actually launch air strikes against land targets is uncertain, because long before continental Europe would be within reach of their own aircraft, the carriers would be under heavy attack from Soviet land-based bombers. The huge American carriers would probably be able to absorb several conventional hits, but a single nuclear blow could be lethal.

Soviet naval strategy and capabilities place considerable emphasis on nuclear strikes to overcome enemy naval forces. Any decision to cross the nuclear threshold, whether on land or at sea, remains a momentous one and is no doubt so regarded by the Soviet leaders. But they might believe that opting to use nuclear weapons at sea would be less escalatory and thus less hazardous. It would certainly offer a possibility of winning the sea battle despite the relative inferiority of their naval forces.

NATO countries view maritime warfare in more conventional terms. Their naval forces, mainly those of the United States, do have some nuclear capability, but it does not play such a prominent role as on the Soviet side. This difference in emphasis can to some extent be explained by the fact that the Warsaw Pact is less likely than NATO to gain the upper hand at sea without resort to nuclear weapons. Taken together, NATO countries have more capable naval forces, and their

29. Notably the AS–3, AS–4, AS–5 and AS–6. The anti-ship ALCMs are basically the same as those for ground attack.

anti-ship missiles are technologically more advanced. Cruise missiles like the 'Harpoon' and the 'Tomahawk', the latter of which will start being introduced into the US Navy in 1984, are quite adequate against the numerous but generally smaller Soviet warships when equipped with a charge of conventional high explosives. US aircraft-carriers, on the other hand, are difficult to sink with conventional munitions. They do form attractive nuclear targets.

As we saw in Chapter 3, Soviet writings on military strategy devote much attention to the advantages of launching a sudden pre-emptive strike. The Soviet Navy does not have the endurance to sustain a lengthy struggle on the high seas. But with its many cruise missiles it could probably inflict serious damage on Western navies if it were to strike by surprise at the onset of a conflict. If executed with nuclear weapons, such a surprise attack could be decisive — all the more so since such a large portion of NATO's naval power is concentrated in the carrier battle groups.

To summarise, the Soviet Navy has undergone spectacular growth. It is probable that it could seriously disrupt Western sea lines of communication, and that it would stand a good chance of keeping NATO fleets away from the land battle. Nevertheless, the maritime balance would still favour the West as long as the conflict remained conventional; it could tilt towards the East once it turned nuclear.

Implications for NATO strategy

The outcome of the Cuban missile crisis is likely to have brought home to the Kremlin leaders some of their relative military weaknesses. Since then, they have managed, by means of unabated efforts, gradually to shift the overall military balance in their favour. The changes in the 'correlation of forces' emboldened the Soviet Union to follow a more active policy of expansion, especially in unstable regions of the Third World; the interventions by proxy in Angola and Ethiopia and the direct intervention in Afghanistan bear witness to this. In addition, it altered some of the basic tenets of deterrence.

The emergence of the Soviet Union as a nuclear power

forced NATO to abandon its strategy of massive retaliation, which implied an almost automatic use of the nuclear sword in case of aggression, and replace it with a strategy offering better possibilities for the avoidance, or at least the deferment, of the engagement of nuclear weapons. As the Soviet Union achieved parity at the strategic level and superiority at the theatre nuclear level, deterrence of conventional aggression through the threat of the initial use of nuclear weapons became less credible. Unlike before, nuclear firepower could no longer be seen as a compensation for conventional deficiencies; rather, the contrary. As the East has more powerful TNF, and since its larger conventional forces are in a better position to absorb nuclear blows, it is doubtful whether recourse to nuclear weapons would improve NATO's situation militarily. Thus NATO's nuclear threshold is much higher at present than it used to be, and as the result, the importance of the conventional balance has increased. These developments affect not only the interface between the conventional and the nuclear level, but also that between the theatre and the strategic level.

The strategic arsenals of the two superpowers, being roughly equal, in a sense tend to nullify each other, a situation which to a certain extent the SALT process formalised. In such a situation the unfavourable balance of substrategic forces (i.e. theatre nuclear and conventional) acquires added significance. It is in the very category of weapons which could be decisive if strategic weapons were not brought into play, namely long-range TNF, that the Soviets have made the greatest strides. At the same time, NATO's comparatively modest capabilities in that field have become less effective, because of the declining ability of aircraft to penetrate Soviet air defences. Thus cracks began to appear in the arch of deterrence, precisely at the juncture between its tactical and strategic stones — a process often termed 'decoupling'.

Europe had been living throughout the 1960s under the shadow of the overwhelming quantity of Soviet continental-range bombers and missiles. These were at the time amply compensated for by American strategic superiority. The situation was in fact considered comfortable enough for NATO, between 1963 and 1965, to dismantle unilaterally its entire

LRTNF, consisting then of 'Thor' and 'Jupiter' land-based missiles and B–47 bombers.

Although strategic parity had become a fact in the 1970s, the Soviet Union went ahead with the introduction of new continental systems like the SS–20 and 'Backfire'. This made it clear that superiority in the European theatre was not just meant to compensate for strategic deficiencies, but was regarded by the Soviet leaders as an end in itself. The massive investment made in forces which are specifically aimed at Europe and only indirectly threaten the United States, points to hegemonic aspirations towards the continent.

The theatre nuclear systems the Soviets are now fielding give a new dimension to the threat to Europe. The new systems, incorporating modern technologies, are highly accurate, and consequently carry lower-yield warheads. This gives the Soviet Union a counter-force potential within the European theatre, which it did not previously have. Highly accurate 'surgical' strikes with SS–20 and shorter-range missiles could eliminate most of NATO's conventional and theatre nuclear armoury in one surprise blow, leaving NATO with no appropriate response — except at the strategic level. The Soviets might come to believe, however wrongly, that they could strike with such discrimination that NATO Europe would be practically disarmed, without causing such collateral damage as to justify strategic retaliation. Such a misperception might be engendered by the thought that the American President would hesitate to cross the strategic threshold for the reason that the Soviets could easily match whatever step he might take. Because no serious threat would be presented by the few NATO theatre systems capable of reaching Soviet territory that would survive — if any survived — a Soviet first strike, a theatre nuclear war might under certain circumstances not be perceived any longer as an unacceptable risk by the Soviet leadership.

Any erosion of deterrence is difficult to quantify, because it ultimately depends on assumptions about Soviet perceptions. Even more difficult to assess in concrete terms is the point at which Soviet power on the continent becomes so overwhelming as to make Western Europe liable to coercion and nuclear blackmail. Various more subtle forms of pressure are already being exerted, examples of which are given in Chapter 8.

The concern over the continuing credibility of deterrence at the theatre level and the possibility of greater susceptibility to various forms of pressure lie behind NATO's December 1979 modernisation decision, which is dealt with in the last chapter.

5

ARMS CONTROL AND DISARMAMENT

Previous chapters described how NATO pursues peace and security by maintaining deterrence and defence capabilities, and stressed the need for an overall balance of forces. In addition, peace and security are pursued through efforts aimed at improving international relations, especially those between East and West, and at reducing the vast quantities of weapons which are piling up in the world.

Efforts to ease tension and initiate mutual restraint in armaments started tentatively in the 1950s and developed more fully in the 1960s. NATO involvement in those efforts was stimulated by the report on 'The Future Tasks of the Alliance' prepared in 1967 by the Belgian Foreign Minister Pierre Harmel and approved by the North Atlantic Council. The report emphasised the dual function of the Alliance:

The Atlantic Alliance has two main functions. Its first function is to maintain adequate military strength and political solidarity to deter aggression and other forms of pressure and to defend the territory of member-countries if aggression should occur. Since its inception, the Alliance has successfully fulfilled this task. But the possibility of a crisis cannot be excluded as long as the central political issues in Europe, first and foremost the German Question, remain unsolved. Moreover, the situation of instability and uncertainty still precludes a balanced reduction of military forces. Under these conditions, the Allies will maintain, as necessary, a suitable military capability to assure the balance of forces, thereby creating a climate of stability, security and confidence.

In this climate the Alliance can carry out its *second function, to pursue the search for progress towards a more stable relationship in which the underlying political issues can be solved. Military security and a policy of détente are not contradictory but complementary.* Collective defence is a stabilising factor in world politics. It is the necessary condition for effective policies directed towards a greater relaxation of tensions. The way to peace and stability in Europe rests in particular on the use of the Alliance constructively in the interest of détente. The participation of the USSR and the USA will be necessary to achieve a settlement of the political problems of Europe.[30]

It would take us too far to discuss détente and East-West relations in general. This chapter focuses on one aspect, the arms control process; but it is good to bear in mind the interconnection between arms control efforts and the East-West relations in general. A chill in those relations, such as set in following the Soviet intervention in Afghanistan, is bound to have a negative impact on the arms control process. But an improvement in East-West relations can ease arms control negotiations. Conversely, the successful conclusion of arms control agreements, enhancing mutual security, would have a beneficial effect on the overall relationship.

Since the Harmel report, the Alliance has pursued an increasingly active arms control policy. Many initiatives were taken either by the Alliance collectively (e.g. MBFR) or by individual members (e.g. SALT). Arms control considerations have also increasingly been integrated into NATO defence planning, especially in relation to nuclear weapons.

Already in the late 1950s, talks took place in pursuit of 'general and complete disarmament under effective international control', the goal set by the United Nations General Assembly. It soon became clear, however, that this was a very distant objective, and that there would only be any hope of attaining it (if such a hope was indeed realistic at all) after many intermediate disarmament steps had been taken and a very different climate had been created from that which then characterised international relations — and does still. Thus a less ambitious approach emerged: *arms control*. Whereas disarmament assumes actual reductions in the amount of weapons and ultimately their complete elimination, arms control seeks the more easily attainable goal of channelling the arms race into a safer course and establishing a more stable balance of power, if possible at lower levels of armaments.

30. Text in 'The North Atlantic Treaty Organisation — Facts and Figures' (NATO Information Service).

Although arms control and disarmament negotiations are slow in yielding results, the achievements so far have been far from negligible, particularly when the fundamental political and ideological differences that still divide East and West are borne in mind. Agreements have been reached on the following, among other things:
— a ban on nuclear weapon tests in the atmosphere (1963);
— the use of outer space (1967);
— the non-proliferation of nuclear weapons (1968);
— a ban of all biological weapons (1972); and
— strategic arms limitations (1972 and 1979).
In addition, there have been negotiations on a variety of other issues, which, it can be hoped, will lead in the future to further agreements. These include:
— a ban on the *possession* of chemical weapons (the *use* of such weapons has been forbidden since 1925);
— mutual and balanced force reductions in Central Europe (see the section on MBFR);
— substantial reductions in intermediate-range nuclear forces;
— measures to halt the burgeoning arms race in outer space (satellite killers etc.).
The scope of the arms control process is gradually expanding. It has come to include quite diverse elements:
— arms control and disarmament in the nuclear, chemical, conventional and other fields;
— co-operation to enhance crisis stability (e.g. hot line agreements);
— confidence- and security-building measures (e.g. notification of manoeuvres, invitation of observers etc.). At the CSCE (Conference on Security and Co-operation in Europe) follow-up meeting in Madrid, the French proposed that a 'Conference on Disarmament in Europe' be held, which would in the first instance seek agreement on such measures.
— international law applicable to armed conflicts (protection of civilians and other humanitarian regulations).
The willingness of the Alliance to engage in a broad dialogue was expressed in the communiqué of the December 1981 ministerial meeting: 'The Allies offer the Soviet Union *comprehensive* negotiations with the aim of effective arms control and disarmament.'

As the arms control process broadens, it becomes more important to consider the interplay between the various agreements and negotiations and their relation to overall security policies. Arms control should not only be a *broad* process but also an *integrated* one. The overall view makes it possible to set priorities and tackle first the most destabilising qualitative or quantitative developments. It also enables the identification of areas of military competition, which have so far remained outside the arms control process but ought to be incorporated into it. One of these 'uncharted areas' is formed by the nuclear short-range systems on the European continent. The Soviet Union is on the verge of replacing its entire short-range arsenal; therefore it seems worth trying to agree on limiting the new Soviet systems (SS–21s and others) and comparable NATO systems before they have been fielded in great numbers.

From its experience in connection with arms control over the past decades, Western thinking has developed a body of interrelated principles relevant to most arms control efforts.

Balance. The foremost principle is that the outcome of arms control and disarmament measures should be a balanced one. If a situation could be achieved where both sides are of about equal strength, aggression would offer little chance of success and so neither side would have reason to fear the other. The principle was laid down already in the 1961 McCloy-Zorin agreement (named after the US and Soviet UN representatives), which stated that all disarmament measures 'should be balanced so that at no stage . . . could any state or group of states gain military advantage, and that security is ensured equally for all'. In practice, this means that where a balance already exists, it suffices to bring it down to a lower level through equal reductions. However, where a balance is lacking, negotiations are much more complicated, because in order to establish a balance at lower levels, the superior side has to accept larger reductions. The problems that can arise in such a situation are illustrated in the MBFR section.

Reciprocity. Both sides are expected to accept significant limitations on their military means. This is the principle of reciprocity or mutuality. The arms race cannot be halted by one side alone.

A small unilateral step can serve as a goodwill gesture by one side towards the other. In 1979, for example, NATO withdrew 1,000 nuclear warheads from Europe. Substantial unilateral disarmament by NATO could, however, be interpreted by Soviet leaders as a sign of weakness and give rise to dangerous miscalculations. If carried beyond a certain point, it would upset the power balance and have destabilising effects. Moreover, unilateral disarmament would remove the incentive to the Soviet Union to seek agreement on two-way arms control measures.

Unilateralists argue that NATO collectively, or member-nations individually, should set a good example. This raises two questions. First, is it reasonable to expect the Soviets to reciprocate? And secondly, what happens if they do not?

In fact, NATO countries have on different occasions shown unilateral restraint or even taken unilateral measures. These were often motivated by budgetary deficits (like the removal of the larger British aircraft-carriers) but sometimes by arms control considerations as well. In the 1970s, for example, the United States deliberately refrained from increasing the number of their nuclear launchers and slowed down the pace of modernisation (see pp. 42 and 51), expecting the Soviets to follow suit. None of these measures has had any effect on the momentum of the Soviet build-up (compare also the decrease in US defence spending in the 1970s with the steady increase on the Soviet side, shown in Chart 4). Thus experience up to the present affords little hope that unilateralism would be reciprocated in the future.

The Soviet Union has always rejected unilateralism when applied to its own forces. Andropov, soon after succeeding as Party leader, reiterated this stance on 22 November 1982 before the CPSU Central Committee: 'Let no one expect unilateral disarmament from us. We are not naive people.'

Stability. The principle of stability is closely related to that of balance. An unbalanced military situation is often unstable because the stronger side will more easily be tempted to exploit its advantage and the weaker side will feel insecure. A balanced situation, on the other hand, is usually also stable and affords the best chance of keeping the peace. However this is not necessarily always the case. One can imagine a situation which is balanced and yet unstable: for example, if the two sides possess the same amount of nuclear weapons but each is also capable of knocking out all the weapons of the other in one strike. This illustrates the paramount importance of having force structures on both sides that generate stability. Stability is provided at present by the existence of secure retaliatory capabilities. Developments that threaten these retaliatory capabilities are destabilising — the deployment of large numbers of highly accurate MIRVed ICBMs is a case in point. It is a priority task of arms control to curb such developments.

Military significance. If arms control measures are to improve mutual security and confidence, they must be militarily significant, i.e. they must really limit the military capabilities of each side, especially those elements which are considered most threatening. Declaratory measures merely add to the stream of words that has already been devoted to the cause of disarmament without really improving the situation. Priority should therefore be given to concrete measures rather than to impressive but unsubstantiated declarations.

Merely cosmetic measures do not meet the criterion of military significance either. The various Soviet proposals on intermediate-range systems (see pp. 111–16) are a case in point. These proposals all portend either a mere displacement of systems like the SS–20 behind the Urals, from where they can still easily reach Western Europe, or the dismantling of obsolescent systems without in any way hampering their replacement by highly capable new systems.

Openness. Each party should make available the information about its own forces needed for negotiating and concluding an agreement. Exaggerated secretiveness will hamper negotiations (see the MBFR section, pp. 71 ff) and will in general breed suspicion. Each party should also allow sufficient openness to enable the other to verify, with adequate confidence, compliance with the terms agreed upon.

The principle of openness also has a wider application. Openness with regard to military matters (e.g. the timely announcement of weapon procurement decisions, the prior notification of manoeuvres etc.) can avoid misperceptions and reduce the uncertainties, which are one of the causes of the arms race and could even be the cause of war.

Verification. A pre-requisite for any arms control agreement is that compliance with its provisions can be adequately verified. A nation that feels it needs armed forces for its security cannot be expected to accept limitations on its forces without being able to ascertain that the other party is keeping its part of the bargain. It is usually the West that insists on including verification provisions in arms control agreements, because it is much more difficult to gather the necessary information in the closed societies of the East than in Western democracies. The Soviet Union recognises the importance of verification, but has shown great reservations about its more intrusive forms, such as on-site inspection, that are sometimes necessary.

The above, of course, forms a typically Western view of arms control and disarmament. The Soviets' outlook on arms control and disarmament is, like the whole of their foreign policy, coloured by ideology. To the Soviet authorities arms control, like peaceful co-existence, is a modified form of struggle, not a road to reconciliation. Certainly, the Soviet leaders accept the need to avoid nuclear war if possible, and they value the contribution made by arms control to crisis stability. But to them negotiations are also a means to realise further overall policy aims, such as driving a wedge between the United States and Western Europe and weakening Western military power wherever possible and especially in Europe. Activities in the field of arms control are fully integrated with other foreign policy instruments such as propaganda. Soviet authorities have no qualms about launching disarmament proposals which are either patently one-sided or merely declaratory, if they believe this will assist them in the propaganda battle or increase the pressure on the Western military establishment. This is not to say that the Soviets never negotiate seriously. In forums like SALT and MBFR they have shown themselves willing to make concessions at a certain juncture, albeit after patient and hard bargaining.

It has been pointed out that despite ongoing negotiations or first step agreements (like SALT), the Soviet military build-up has continued unabated. This is fully in line with the notion entertained by the Soviet authorities that arms control agreements are concessions wrung out of the West by the growth of their military power. Accordingly, a military build-up, far from endangering world peace, is seen as creating favourable conditions for détente and arms control.[31]

It would be beyond the scope of this work to cover all present arms control forums. The following sections will deal with SALT and MBFR. The negotiations on Intermediate-Range Nuclear Forces (INF) will be described in the final chapter.

From SALT to START

The 'Strategic Arms Limitations Talks' (SALT) between the United States and the Soviet Union are seen by many as the corner-stone of the whole arms control process. Although the talks have so far hardly led to any actual reductions, they are nevertheless considered of fundamental importance because they have brought greater predictability and stability to the strategic balance between the superpowers.

Following three years of negotiations, two agreements (SALT I) were reached in 1972. Of these, one froze the amount of ICBMs and SLBMs on both sides, and the other banned Anti-Ballistic Missile (ABM) defences almost entirely. Subsequent negotiations (SALT II) expanded the limits on ICBMs and SLBMs and covered long–range bombers also. However, the treaty signed in 1979 was never ratified by the US Senate.

SALT has generally focused on central systems, but some other systems have been discussed too. As soon as the SALT I negotiations had started in 1969, the Soviets demanded that what they described as US 'Forward-Based Systems' be included in the limits. The term 'Forward-Based Systems' (FBS) comprises all US systems which, though not of inter-continental range, are nevertheless deployed in such a way as to be able to reach Soviet territory. The US systems listed by

31. For a comparison of Western and Eastern attitudes towards arms control see Laurence Martin, 'The Two-Edged Sword' (Reith Lecture), *The Listener*, December 1981.

the Soviets under this heading vary. Generally they include carrier-based aircraft, the F–111 (based in Britain and West Germany) and the F–4 'Phantom' (which, even from its West German bases, is not in fact capable of making two-way missions over Soviet territory). It should be noted that the Soviets were not at the same time offering to limit *their* systems which threaten NATO Europe but not the United States. What the FBS concept implied was that the systems that can reach Soviet territory from Western Europe are important, but those that can reach Western Europe from the Soviet Union are not. In addition the Soviets claimed that British and French SLBMs should be taken into account.

The United States refused to discuss the so-called FBS and third-country (i.e. French and British) systems, arguing that the talks were confined to the central balance between the superpowers and that they were not entitled to negotiate for other countries. The Europeans, fearing that their interests might be sacrificed, did not favour inclusion of FBS at the time (now the situation is entirely different, since the substrategic systems of *both* the United States and the Soviet Union are the subject of special talks). Great Britain and France have always refused to subject their comparatively small nuclear forces to any limitations.

To compensate for the exclusion of FBS and third-country systems from SALT I, the Soviets insisted that they were entitled to maintain *more* central systems than the United States. The SALT I treaty did in the end contain unequal ceilings, not so much as a compensation for FBS or third-country systems, but because the ceilings basically froze the existing force ratios, which favoured the Soviet Union as far as launchers were concerned. A breakthrough was achieved on this matter during the SALT II negotiations when, at the Vladivostok summit in 1974, Brezhnev accepted the principle of equal ceilings on all central systems (ICBMs, SLBMs and long-range bombers) and agreed to drop the FBS question.

The SALT II negotiations were complicated by the emergence of 'grey area' systems. On the American side these were new-generation cruise missiles. US negotiators initially contended that cruise missiles did not fall under the terms agreed at Vladivostok, but in the end they agreed to count bombers equipped with ALCMs against the MIRV ceiling, and to have some temporary limitations on GLCMs and SLCMs.

The Soviet 'Backfire' bomber proved an equally difficult issue. The United States wanted to include the aircraft in the ceilings because it considers it to have some intercontinental strike capability, but the Soviets maintained that it was a medium-range bomber and refused to include it. They did, however, provide assurances that no measures would be taken that would allow the 'Backfire' to operate at intercontinental distances. Furthermore they agreed to limit production to its current rate of thirty units a year.

The SALT II treaty, which was solemnly signed by President Carter and Leonid Brezhnev on 18 June 1979, ran into trouble in the US Senate. Several elements of the treaty aroused criticism: the handling of the 'Backfire' issue, the formalisation of the Soviet monopoly of heavy ICBMs, and above all the insufficient limitations on the MIRVing of Soviet ICBMs. The latter was a consequence of the fact that the ceilings were set at rather high levels and were expressed in terms of launchers, leaving warheads almost unconstrained. This enabled the Soviet Union to continue placing new MIRVed ICBMs in the field, virtually to the point of acquiring a first-strike capability against the United States ICBM force. The Carter administration pointed out that the treaty did contain some significant limitations: the Soviets would be forced to dismantle 250 systems and would not be allowed to increase the current number of MIRVs per existing type of missile. It argued that the United States would be worse off without the treaty.

President Carter had tried to get the Soviet Union to agree to more significant reductions of ICBMs. Proposals involving 'deep cuts' were made in March 1977, but were rejected out of hand. The Carter administration then reverted to the Vladivostok framework, although it managed to get Soviet agreement on some further limitations.

The Soviet intervention in Afghanistan interrupted the SALT II ratification process in the US Senate, the outcome of which was already uncertain. It was, in fact, never resumed, and a new administration came to power which considered

SALT II to be 'fundamentally flawed'. President Reagan decided to start new negotiations. To underline the need for sizeable reductions, they were renamed 'Strategic Arms *Reduction* Talks' (START). Having taken steps to modernise US strategic forces, the Reagan administration proceeds from the assumption that it has the leverage which its predecessor lacked to induce the Soviets to accept deep cuts. The talks began on 29 June 1982 in Geneva. The US aim in START, as enunciated by President Reagan in a speech which he made at Eureka College on 9 May 1982, is 'to enhance deterrence and achieve stability through significant reductions in the most destabilising nuclear systems, ballistic missiles, and especially intercontinental ballistic missiles'.

Accordingly the United States wants to focus initial negotiating efforts on large cuts in both land-based and sea-based ballistic missiles. To this end it has proposed:
— an aggregate ceiling of 5,000 on ICBM and SLBM warheads;
— a subceiling of 2,500 on ICBM warheads alone; and
— an aggregate ceiling of 850 on deployed ICBM and SLBM missiles.
A significant departure from SALT is that *warheads* have replaced *launchers* as the main unit of limitation. Because warheads are a better measure of military capability, this is a logical step. Furthermore it is precisely in the field of MIRVs that the most dynamic developments are taking place. The ceiling of 5,000 on warheads would force both sides to cut down the number of ICBM and SLBM warheads by about one-third (for current figures, see Table 5). The ceiling of 850 on ICBMs and SLBMs would force the United States to halve its ballistic missile force. The Soviet Union, which maintains a larger missile force, would have to reduce by even more.

In a later stage the United States proposes the imposition of equal limits on the aggregate throw-weight of strategic missiles. The Soviet Union, because of the larger size of its missiles, has an enormous advantage in this respect and can therefore in the first instance be expected to resist limits on throw-weight.

The United States considers the limiting of 'slow-flying' systems (i.e. bombers and cruise missiles) a less urgent task because these systems could not be used for a first strike. However, the United States declared that all systems are negotiable, and it expressed willingness to accept equal ceilings on bombers, which would also automatically limit ALCMs.

In its first reaction to the American proposals, the Soviet Union complained that a provision permitting only half the number of missile warheads to be mounted on ICBMs required it to make great changes in its force structure, whereas US forces would hardly be affected — 72 per cent of all Soviet strategic warheads are on ICBMs and only 19 per cent are on SLBMs; in the United States less than 25 per cent are on ICBMs and 51 per cent on SLBMs. Such objections are understandable, but overall stability would benefit from the proposed shift from land to sea. When deployed in large numbers, modern MIRVed ICBMs pose a first-strike threat to the ICBMs of the other side. Current SLBMs do not have a hard target kill capability — their warheads are too small and not accurate enough. Furthermore, SLBMs have a great advantage over ICBMs in that they are much less vulnerable. As the United States proceeds with the M-X, a new ICBM that will significantly add to its hard target capability, the Soviets are likely to come to regard their heavy reliance on ICBMs as a liability. A shift towards the less vulnerable sea-based missiles would then be the logical course for them. In fact, the launching of the *Typhoon*, the first of a new class of gigantic strategic submarines, might signify the first step in that direction.

The greater symmetry between US and Soviet forces resulting from a Soviet shift from land-based to sea-based missiles would also facilitate further arms control efforts in the strategic field. The new stability provided by the three ceilings would, if these were agreed upon, be further enhanced if the two sides were also to agree on measures to prevent coming generations of SLBMs from being given the capability to knock out ICBM silos.

The Soviets have put forward proposals of their own. Already before START got under way, Brezhnev suggested in a speech to the Komsomol on 18 May 1982 that the strategic armaments of both parties should be frozen quantitatively and to some extent also qualitatively right from the start of the talks. This was rejected by the United States because it would have ratified the Soviet strategic build-up of the past decade, while preventing US measures to remedy some of the resulting vulnerabilities. A freeze would in fact leave the Soviet Union little incentive to negotiate actual force reductions seriously. The United States argued, furthermore, that reaching agreement on the details of a freeze would be just as complicated as a real reduction agreement and would thus divert the negotiators from the latter more compelling task.

In the first round of negotiations, the Soviets proposed an aggregate ceiling of 1,800 on ICBMs, SLBMs and heavy bombers. This would be an improvement over SALT II, where they refused to go below 2,250, but it falls short of the American reduction goal. Ballistic missiles and bombers are lumped together in the proposed ceiling, as in SALT II. However, the distinction between these two is fundamental to the new US approach. Ballistic missiles have a short flight-time and 100 per cent penetration probability, whereas bombers and cruise missiles have a long flight-time and are vulnerable to air defence. A complicating factor is that the Soviets have tied reductions of the strategic arsenals to limitations on US substrategic systems; they require for the duration of the agreement a freeze of US 'Forward-Based Systems' including the non-deployment of GLCMs and Pershing II missiles in Europe.

The Soviet willingness to go further than SALT II is in itself an encouraging sign. The negotiations will certainly not be easy, however, and it could take some time before they yield results. Meanwhile both sides continue to act upon their respective declarations to abide by the terms of the formally expired SALT I treaty. The United States is also respecting the unratified SALT II treaty. The Soviet Union has not dismantled the 250 systems it has in excess of the SALT II ceilings, but appears to be complying with the other provisions of the treaty.

MBFR

Since 1973, negotiations have been going on in Vienna

between NATO and the Warsaw Pact about 'Mutual and Balanced Force Reductions' (MBFR) in the area Benelux–West Germany on the one side and East Germany–Poland–Czechoslovakia on the other side. The Western participants seek through these negotiations to establish a more balanced situation at lower levels of forces in Central Europe, in conjunction with a set of measures designed to ensure compliance with the agreement and to make military activities more transparent, thereby improving mutual confidence. The negotiations have not yet led to concrete results, but the distance between Eastern and Western positions has narrowed appreciably in the course of the negotiations.

At first, East and West advocated entirely different methods to reduce troops. Western participants proposed that ground forces be cut down in such a way that only 700,000 men would be left on each side in the area. Because the Warsaw Pact has more troops in the reduction area, it would therefore have to withdraw/disband more men to reach the 700,000 common collective ceiling. The West argued that this was a fair proposal because, with equal numbers on both sides, each would remain capable of defending itself without presenting a threat to the other. In addition, it was pointed out that US troops withdrawn would have to return across the Atlantic, whereas Soviet troops would have to be moved a relatively short distance since their homeland borders on the reduction area.

The Eastern participants proposed a different method: reductions by equal percentages. The Western participants rejected this approach because it would contractually fix the present imbalance and place the West in a position of permanent inferiority.

In 1978 the East accepted the idea of a common ceiling at 700,000. This was less of a concession than it may seem, because the East maintained its assertion that there already existed an approximate balance: it claimed it had only 805,000 ground troops in the area, while NATO estimated that the correct figure was 962,000.[32] Since NATO ground forces

32. The figures are drawn from M. Getler, 'Warsaw Pact's Arithmetic puzzles NATO', *International Herald Tribune*, 28 September 1978.

numbered 791,000, the 700,000 ceiling could be reached, on the basis of Eastern data, by practically equal reductions instead of the asymmetrial reductions needed according to NATO estimates.

Western negotiators proposed to their Eastern counterparts that they should sort out together the discrepancy of over 150,000 men between the figures provided by the East and the Western estimates. They suggested comparing breakdowns of the respective data. The Eastern participants co-operated to some extent at first, but they soon became reluctant to carry on when the discussion started to become more specific. The West provided further breakdowns of its intelligence estimates, but the East failed to follow suit and accused the West of trying to turn disarmament negotiations into an attempt at military espionage. Soviet secretiveness has so far precluded resolution of the data issue, which remains the central stumbling–block in the negotiations.

The importance of removing the uncertainties regarding Eastern data can be illustrated by the sequel provoked in the Vienna talks by the unilateral withdrawal of 20,000 men from East Germany, announced by Brezhnev in October 1979. The unilateral withdrawal was originally part of a broad 'peace offensive' designed to dissuade NATO from its plans to modernise LRTNF. After NATO had decided in December 1979, nevertheless, to deploy new 'Pershings' and GLCMs in Europe, the Soviets demanded that their unilateral withdrawal be credited in MBFR.

Western participants in the MBFR talks asked the Soviets to clarify the net effect of the changes in their manpower strength in the area. Since the unilateral withdrawal had not been submitted to any verification measures, it was difficult for the West to ascertain to what extent the claimed withdrawal had actually taken place. In addition, there was growing evidence that the Soviets had begun to increase the size of their divisions, and this might more than make up for any previous withdrawal. Up to the time of writing, the Soviets have not clarified the net result of their withdrawals and strength increases.

Since the beginning of the talks in 1973 the two sides have made a sizeable number of proposals and counter-proposals.

In July 1982 the West made new comprehensive proposals presented in the form of a draft treaty. These proposals built on previous elements of the Western position and incorporated those elements on which a certain consensus had emerged between East and West. A new factor was that Western participants now offered to lay down all reductions in one single treaty. Until then they had insisted that the two superpowers should first seek an agreement on initial reductions. While implementing the first agreement, a second agreement would be sought that covered further reductions, this time by *all* countries with troops in the area.

Eastern participants have always had a preference for a single treaty. They wanted, at the least, a strong link between the first and second phase; this was because the Soviet Union had misgivings about accepting limitations on its troops in the reduction area in Phase I without the assurance that the West German army would be limited in Phase II. By proposing a single treaty, the West was more than meeting this concern, because all countries involved would now be formally committed from the outset to take part in the reductions. The East welcomed this aspect of the Western proposals, but the data problem and the Eastern reluctance to accept the associated measures needed for verification continue to stand in the way of agreement in Vienna.

6
REFINEMENTS OF US/NATO STRATEGY

'Should a President, in the event of a nuclear attack, be left with the single option of ordering the mass destruction of enemy civilians, in the face of the certainty that it would be followed by the mass slaughter of Americans?'

With this rhetorical question, President Nixon was admitting in 1970[33] that the threat of assured destruction was in fact unlikely to be implemented in response to a limited attack on military targets causing few civilian casualties. Retaliation against urban-industrial targets deterred only a narrow range of extreme contingencies. To remedy the lack of flexibility in strategic targeting, the US Defense Secretary, James R. Schlesinger, introduced *selective* counter-force options into planning from 1974 onwards. The policy was not really new; as long before as 1961, part of the strategic forces had been retargeted from urban-industrial to military objectives. The difference lay in the emphasis which was now put on the smaller scale of the counter-force options. Schlesinger's concept of 'selective nuclear options' was applied to TNF operational planning as well.

The efforts to provide more flexibility involved not just planning but also weapon procurement. Greater stress was laid on the ability to conduct discriminate attacks causing as little *collateral* (i.e. non-military) damage as possible, especially with regard to theatre weapons. Higher accuracy and lower yields were part of the answer, as improved guidance techniques made it possible to obtain the same military effect with a smaller warhead. Another method consisted of tailoring the explosive device to the characteristics of the target to be destroyed (tanks, concrete bunkers etc.). This can be done by varying the proportions of energy which a nuclear explosion releases in the form of blast, heat and initial

33. In 'US Foreign Policy for the 1970s: a Report to Congress'.

and residual radiation[34] respectively, so as to maximise military efficiency and minimise collateral damage. The best-known example is the 'Reduced Blast/Enhanced Radiation' warhead, better known as the 'neutron bomb'.

In 1980 the process of refining the flexible response concept was carried a step further, when President Carter signed Presidential Directive 59 (PD–59), which codifies the doctrine of United States strategic forces as it had evolved in previous years. Although a new name — 'countervailing strategy' — was coined, the concept could hardly be considered new, as is clear from the description of it given by former US Defense Secretary Harold Brown:

> We have concluded that if deterrence is to be fully effective, the United States must be able to respond at a level appropriate to the type and scale of a Soviet attack. Our goal is to make a Soviet victory as improbable (seen through Soviet eyes) as we can make it, over the broadest plausible range of scenarios. We must therefore have plans for attacks which pose a more credible threat than an all-out attack on Soviet industry and cities. These plans should include options to attack the targets that comprise the Soviet military force structure and political power structure, and to hold back a significant reserve. In other words, we must be able to deter Soviet attacks of less than all-out scale by making it clear to the Kremlin that, after such an attack, we would not be forced to the stark choice of either making no effective military response or totally destroying the Soviet Union. We could instead attack, in a selective and measured way, a range of military, industrial, and political control targets, while retaining an assured destruction capacity in reserve.[35]

'Pure deterrence' versus 'deterrence through defence'

The development of Western strategic thinking since the late

34. Initial radiation is emitted by the ball of fire in the minutes following the explosion. Residual radiation occurs later and, on the whole, indirectly (fall-out).

35. Harold Brown, Secretary of Defense, 'Annual Report FY 1981', p. 66.

1950s can be viewed as a gradual movement away from 'pure deterrence', as embodied in the concept of massive retaliation, towards greater flexibility and a 'compartmentalisation' of the escalation process; a doctrinal evolution that was made necessary by the shifting nuclear balance. The increase in flexibility was made possible by the dynamic quality of American research efforts, which began to yield in the 1970s the technology needed to create counter-force options. Proponents of greater flexibility were confirmed in their thinking by the fact that the Soviet Union was acquiring a counter-force capability too. Technologically the Soviets lagged behind in such crucial areas as precision guidance, but conceptually they had incorporated the counter-force calculus into their nuclear strategy long before the Americans. For Soviet strategists, very much influenced as they are by traditional military thinking, it is natural to take the destruction of enemy forces (whether conventional or nuclear) as the key objective. They have never shared the focus on deterrence which characterises Western thinking.

TNF modernisation and developments in US strategic thought, such as the Schlesinger doctrine and PD–59, have raised concern in some areas of European public opinion that the United States would contemplate conducting a protracted nuclear war limited to Europe, while insulating its own territory from nuclear devastation. According to this line of reasoning, a much-reduced nuclear stockpile in Western Europe would strengthen rather than harm deterrence, since it would signal a readiness to escalate rapidly to the strategic level. The suggestion that the United States would be willing to fight a prolonged nuclear war at Europe's expense has been rejected by Americans — sometimes indignantly — as a 'disgusting claim' that 'ignores the several hundreds of thousands of American troops stationed in Europe who would also be victims of such a conflict'.[36] In addition it was pointed out that it has been a constant aim of the Soviet Union to separate Europe's security from that of the United States, so as to be in the position to use or threaten to use nuclear weapons against

36. Assistant Secretary of State Lawrence Eagleburger, address before North Atlantic Assembly, 15 October 1981.

NATO Europe without incurring any serious risks to its own territory.

It is a fact that the drive to compartmentalise deterrence originated in the United States, this being clearly in its interest. The question is whether swinging the pendulum back towards 'pure' deterrence is a sensible alternative or in the interest of Europeans. The present debate over 'pure deterrence' versus 'deterrence through defence capability' is basically a repetition of the debate between the proponents of 'massive retaliation' and 'flexible response', conducted in the early 1960s. The conclusion then was that the growth of Soviet nuclear capabilities had made the massive retaliation concept either ineffectual or, if it was still taken seriously, highly dangerous for Americans and Europeans *alike*. This reasoning is even more valid today since the Soviets have acquired not only at least a comparable quantity of nuclear weapons but also the capability to carry out limited, pinpoint counter-force strikes. Henry Kissinger once said in this connection:

> 'I believe that the side whose only strategic option is to target the civilian population and the industrial capacity of its opponent, and which can define no military objective, will be relying on a strategy that will be psychologically and politically almost untenable — especially if it is also inferior in forces for local intervention. Every calculation with which I am familiar indicates that a general nuclear war in which civilian populations are the primary target will produce casualties exceeding 100 million. Such a degree of devastation is not a strategic doctrine; it is an abdication of moral and political responsibility. No political structure could survive it. . . .
>
> 'I am quite willing to accept the proposition that our retaliatory capability is enormous, but if the only probable targets are civilians it will nevertheless leave us politically paralysed.'[37]

It has been pointed out that if the logic of the flexible response strategy were carried to its extremes, NATO would

37. Interview in *The Economist*, 3 February 1979.

have to match the Warsaw Pact at every rung of the escalation ladder. Parity at each level (leaving aside the idea of superiority) would in theory seem to offer the best conditions for effective deterrence, since the Soviets would have no prospect of victory at any level and the risk of escalation would remain present. In practice such a proposition is unrealistic, not to say undesirable, because parity at each level would represent a financial and political burden that could not be demanded of Western democracies. To date, NATO's conventional and theatre nuclear deficiencies have been offset by a correspondingly higher risk of escalation — a risk that has been acknowledged and accepted.

While there is general agreement that a conventional balance is a desirable goal, although one unlikely to be attained, many analysts have guarded against an over-compartmentalised view of the nuclear spectrum, lest NATO should embark on a fruitless attempt to mirror Soviet capabilities. While conceding that the present LRTNF imbalance could have destabilising consequences, it has been stressed that a separate 'Eurostrategic balance' should be avoided, as this could be perceived by the Soviets as a renunciation of the link with US central systems. It should be noted in this respect that even after the installation of the planned 572 GLCMs and 'Pershings', NATO would still have far fewer long-range theatre systems than the Soviet Union, and there could thus be no question of a separate balance.

On 23 March 1983, in what became known as his 'Star Wars' speech, President Reagan unfolded a 'vision of the future' in which the present mutual assured destruction would be replaced by mutual invulnerability. To this end he ordered a long-term research and development programme aimed at developing futuristic defensive systems, such as space–based laser battle stations that could destroy any missile soon after launch. The Soviet Union is carrying out a major research effort of its own in this field. However, Reagan's vision of the future would seem to be attainable only if the Soviets accept his new defensive philosophy and refrain from trying to develop countermeasures. Andropov's highly critical initial reaction offers little hope in this respect, so that an intensification of the arms race seems ultimately to be the more likely outcome.

7

THE NEUTRON BOMB

Public attention was first drawn to the so-called 'neutron bomb' by an article in the *Washington Post* on 6 June 1977. A heated public debate ensued.

Basically, the neutron bomb is just another nuclear weapon adding to the diversity of types already available: no more and no less evil. Like all other nuclear weapons in Western arsenals, its primary function is to deter. Because initially little concrete information was provided as to what the neutron bomb could and could not do, free rein was given to all kinds of horrific stories. Thus the neutron bomb became singled out as an emotional issue in a way that was not to be expected in view of the fact that its similarities to other nuclear weapons are far more significant than its dissimilarities.

Technical features

The 'neutron bomb' is actually a new warhead designed for the 'Lance' missile and for dual-capable artillery. As distinct from present 'atomic' warheads which rely on a *fission* reaction, the neutron warhead relies on *fusion* and is therefore related to the hydrogen bomb.

Compared with existing atomic bombs, the neutron bomb emits more initial radiation but less blast and heat, hence the official denomination 'Reduced Blast/Enhanced Radiation' (RB/ER) weapon. It has been specially designed to counter tanks and other armoured vehicles. Standard fission (i.e. atomic) weapons can be used against tank units too, but the problem with them is that they produce heat and blast in quantities which can be fatal for civilians, especially if unprotected, over a large area. Tanks however will only be affected within a relatively small area around the explosion, where, despite the protective armour, the crews will succumb to the effects of radiation and, to a certain extent, heat. By producing more radiation of a better armour-penetrating quality (i.e. high-energy neutrons) but less of the other effects

80

of a nuclear weapon, the RB/ER warhead produces the maximum tank-stopping power while at the same time producing the minimum of collateral damage.

The distribution of energy released by the explosion compares as shown in the accompanying table. A 1-kiloton RB/ER weapon emits the same amount of radiation as a 10-kiloton standard fission device. The military result is about the same: tanks are put out of action within a radius of

	Standard fission weapon %	ER/RB weapon %
Initial radiation	5	30
Blast	50	40
Heat	35	25
Residual radiation	10	5

approximately 900 m. Thus with a RB/ER feature, yields can be reduced by a factor of 10. Through the combined effects of smaller yields and the suppression of blast and heat, it is possible to reduce substantially the area of collateral damage, while still obtaining the same anti-tank effect. For example, a 10-kiloton atomic burst would still cause first- to second-degree burns on exposed skin at a distance of 3.5 km.; a 1–kiloton RB/ER weapon would not cause such burns beyond 1.1 km. Similarly, there would be a substantial reduction in the distance from ground zero at which blast damage (varying from collapse of buildings to ear-drum rupture) would still occur. The duration and intensity of residual radiation (fall-out) would also be far less. Troops under armoured cover, entering an area one hour after a RB/ER burst, would receive only the minimal dose of 1 or 2 RAD (radiation absorbed dose). For this reason the neutron bomb is sometimes described as a 'clean' nuclear weapon.

The conclusion is inevitable that the neutron bomb is far more *discriminate* than existing atomic bombs. It would enable the number of civilian casualties which are likely to follow an attack against a military target to be significantly reduced. The neutron bomb, like all nuclear weapons, does cause some damage to buildings and other objects, but on a much smaller scale.

Tactical implications

Because the effects of a RB/ER weapon are confined to a relatively small area, the minimum safe distance from one's own troops at which it can be used is shorter than with current fission weapons. This has important tactical implications.

We saw earlier (p. 36) that in order to avoid being exposed to possible nuclear strikes, Warsaw Pact troops are trained to concentrate and engage the enemy very rapidly and to infiltrate his defences. The assumption is that once attacking units are sufficiently close to enemy positions, they can no longer be the object of a nuclear attack as this would put friendly troops at risk too. These Soviet tactics would be foiled by the RB/ER warhead, because it can be used nearer NATO defences. Thus introduction of the RB/ER weapon would force the Warsaw Pact to adopt more decentralised tactics, dispersing its troops more than is currently envisaged. This would facilitate conventional defence.

By the very nature of its radiation, the neutron bomb is of greater utility to a defender than to an attacker. While the high-energy neutrons penetrate armour fairly easily, they are relatively well checked by organic matters like a layer of earth. Consequently, well dug-in defenders are much less vulnerable to a strike with a neutron projectile than are tank units moving up for attack.

Strategic implications

Introduction of the neutron weapon would strengthen deterrence on two accounts. It would do so, first, because it would enable enemy armoured thrusts to be countered more effectively. The fact that a tactical nuclear exchange would be very destructive and, to judge from present force ratios, probably not even to NATO's advantage in a military sense has tended to weaken deterrence at theatre level. The military effectiveness of the RB/ER weapon would improve the situation in this respect.

The second reason why the RB/ER weapon would strengthen overall deterrence lies in the reduced collateral damage it causes. The more discriminate a nuclear weapon is, the more credible appears the threat to use it, especially when friendly territory is involved. This is the paradox of deterrence: the more credible the threat to use a weapon becomes, the better it deters and the smaller the probability that it will ever actually have to be used.

The nuclear threshold

One of the objections that have been raised against the neutron bomb is that it lowers the nuclear threshold. Before analysing this assertion, we have to clarify the concept of threshold.

The nuclear threshold is the combination of elements that induces one of the belligerents in the course of a conflict to make the first use of a nuclear weapon. One can distinguish between the established release procedures (the *formal* threshold), on the one hand, and the considerations taken into account by the decision-makers (the *material* threshold), on the other hand.

What determines the material threshold on the NATO side? This would be, in the first place, the perception by the political leadership of the situation, especially (assuming that the conventional threshold has already been crossed) the tide of the conventional battle. It follows that the stronger NATO conventional defences are, the higher the nuclear threshold will be. Conversely, a deterioration of the conventional balance, as we have been witnessing for over a decade, lowers the nuclear threshold.

Another factor that will doubtless weigh heavily in the minds of decision-makers is the enemy reaction they expect — will it be limited or massive? In the days of the US monopoly of the atom bomb, the nuclear threshold was probably at its all-time low because the Soviet Union could only have responded conventionally. The growth of the Soviet nuclear arsenal gradually raised NATO's nuclear threshold, which as a result is now higher than it ever was before. One can say, at least in theory, that if NATO's nuclear threshold is raised without this being compensated for by a strengthening of conventional defences, deterrence will be correspondingly weakened and the Soviet 'conventional threshold' is likely to be lowered.

The main feature of the formal nuclear threshold, both in Western nuclear powers (the United States, Britain and France) and in the Soviet Union, is that the ultimate decision rests with the highest political authority. Both sides stress the need for political control throughout the escalation process. Fears have been voiced that introduction of the RB/ER weapon would require delegation of release authority from the political to the military level. This would be necessary, it is contended, because NATO's elaborate release procedures would be too time-consuming to cope with time-urgent targets like highly mobile tank units.

Several incorrect assumptions are involved in this line of thought. If NATO, faced with an overwhelming conventional onslaught, decided to cross the nuclear threshold, this would indeed only be done after mature deliberation at the highest political level. Initial use is likely to have primarily a political aim, i.e. to convince the aggressor that he must cease hostilities. Military effectiveness would only be required to the extent necessary to bring about the desired political effect. In such a context, the first nuclear weapon to be used need not be a neutron bomb, nor would such a mobile target as a tank unit have to be selected if this proved difficult. Once nuclear weapons have already been engaged on either side, it should be possible to go through NATO's elaborate release procedure with the required speed. The requirement for absolute political control of course remains.

In any case it is out of the question that an exception to established NATO procedures would be made for the neutron bomb. The need for overall political guidance of military operations, especially when nuclear weapons are involved, is a firmly established principle within NATO. In this connection it should be mentioned that, although the neutron bomb is more discriminate than other nuclear weapons, it nevertheless in no way compares to a conventional weapon. The damage wrought by the explosion would still be measured in kilometres, instead of metres as in the case of conventional explosives.

NATO, as we have seen, has explicitly renounced the

development of weapons such as 'mininukes', which would blur the threshold between the nuclear and the conventional. Thus a clear limit has been set to the miniaturisation of nuclear weapons at the point where the scope of destruction would no longer differ fundamentally from the most powerful conventional weapons.

It should be clear from the foregoing that the formal nuclear threshold will not be affected in any way by the neutron bomb. We shall now turn to the impact on the material threshold.

It has been argued that, since the RB/ER weapon causes less collateral damage, it will be more readily used. This, however, is only one facet of the matter. We saw that the expected Soviet response was one of the main factors determining the material threshold. As there is no reason to assume that the Soviets' reaction to a neutron strike would differ much from their reaction to an atomic strike, in fact nothing changes in that respect.

We saw also that the neutron bomb places at risk even those enemy units that are close to friendly defence positions. Consequently, the attacker is forced to avoid heavy troop concentrations, which in turn eases the task of the defender. This could *raise* the nuclear threshold on the NATO side.

Another factor which might raise the threshold is that having a discriminate weapon like the neutron bomb at hand could reduce the pressure on the defender to halt invading armour *before* it reaches heavily populated areas.

Production decision

By 1977, development of the RB/ER warhead was nearing completion. Although up till then the United States had always taken decisions regarding its nuclear stockpile on its own accord, President Carter made it known that he wanted to consult his Allies beforehand. For the first time, Europeans were in a sense asked to share responsibility for a US production decision. Consultations began in September 1977, but proved inconclusive because most European governments were growing apprehensive about the public controversy surrounding the weapon. The Soviet Union fueled the debate with a coordinated propaganda campaign in which the neutron bomb was depicted as an 'inhumane' and 'barbaric' weapon. The sharp tone of the campaign and the massive effort put into it indicate that the Soviets are well aware of the effectiveness of the RB/ER weapon as a counter to their numerically superior tank force.

When West Germany and Britain had finally come out in favour of the new weapon, President Carter unexpectedly reversed American policy, announcing on 7 April 1978 that he had decided to defer its production:

> 'I have decided to defer production of weapons with enhanced radiation effects. The ultimate decisions regarding the incorporation of enhanced radiation features into our modernised battlefield weapons will be made later, and will be influenced by the degree to which the Soviet Union shows restraint in its conventional and nuclear arms programs and force deployments affecting the security of the United States and Western Europe.'

For the production of the RB/ER warhead to be abandoned altogether, the Soviet Union was expected to restrict its deployment of either SS–20 missiles or tanks threatening Western Europe. In reply, President Brezhnev declared: 'We too will not begin production of neutron arms so long as the United States does not do so.'[38] Any trade-off with existing Soviet weapons was rejected. The United States had already said on an earlier occasion that it did not consider a mutual renunciation of neutron weapons as a serious concession, because such weapons were, in view of their effectiveness against tanks, clearly much more important to the West than to the East.

The postponement of neutron bomb production was a unilateral step. One of the reasons why it was not reciprocated in any meaningful way probably lies in the fact that, because of public opposition in Western Europe, it seemed unlikely at the time that the weapon would ever reach operational status. In such a situation there was little inducement for the Soviet leaders to curtail weapon deployments of their own in return.

The neutron bomb receded from the headlines until the

38. Address to Komsomol Congress, 25 April 1978.

advent of President Reagan, who decided in August 1981 to go ahead with production. Unlike the previous administration, he stressed that production decisions were solely a national US responsibility. Deployment outside US territory was not under consideration. Any decision to that effect would only occur after close consultations with any country on whose territory the weapons would be stationed.

Finally, it should be mentioned that France is developing a neutron device of its own.

8

ARMAMENT AND DISARMAMENT IN THE GREY AREA

The emergence of strategic parity and the appearance of a new generation of Soviet theatre (especially intermediate-range) systems combined to create concern in Western Europe: was the link between Europe's defence and the US strategic nuclear forces being weakened and was deterrence therefore being eroded? One of the earlier expressions of these concerns was Chancellor Helmut Schmidt's Alastair Buchan Memorial Lecture in October 1977 (see page 44). In Europe, and then in the United States, the feeling grew that if the profound change which the Soviet programmes were bringing about in the power balance were simply to be accepted, this could initiate a slide into political paralysis and would, beyond a certain stage, invite nuclear blackmail.

The decisions to deploy the 'Backfire' and SS–20 had been taken in the secrecy of the Kremlin and were only revealed once the first prototypes had been spotted by US satellites. The decision on a NATO response — several years later — was taken under very different conditions. It was the subject of a heated, long-drawn-out debate which would be unthinkable in a totalitarian state. The Soviet authorities did, however, make abundant use of the freedom of speech existing in the West to intervene in the discussion about the new missiles between European governments and their public, as if it were entirely normal for the Soviet Union to have a say on Western defence matters. Initially dicussion focused on the need to redress the growing theatre nuclear disparity and to reaffirm the strategic link between the United States and its Allies. The issue gradually developed into a test of the Alliance's cohesion and its ability to take a decision and carry it through in the face of Soviet pressure and propaganda. To this another problem must be added, which is coming increasingly to the fore: the ability of political leaders to convince the public of the wisdom of their basic policy choices in security matters.

The dual-track approach

The decision to modernise long-range theatre nuclear forces (longer-range INF in the new terminology) was reached after two years of detailed discussion within NATO.

In October 1977, the ministerial meeting of the Nuclear Planning Group (NPG — NATO's main forum for nuclear affairs) established a 'High Level Group' (HLG) whose task was to examine NATO's TNF requirements. In 1978 the HLG reached the conclusion that NATO's LRTNF should be strengthened, and started examining how this could best be done. Another working party, the 'Special Group on Arms Control and Related Matters', was set up by the North Atlantic Council in April 1979 to examine the arms control implications of the recommendations that were being made by the HLG.

In September 1979, the two working groups concluded their studies. During the NPG meeting in November 1979, defence ministers reviewed the results and

> . . . considered the urgent requirement for modernizing NATO theatre nuclear forces as part of the Long Term Defence Programme and the parallel need for related arms control measures. In this context, ministers noted that the modernization of theatre nuclear systems would, by adding highly accurate and survivable long-range systems based in NATO Europe, enhance NATO's deterrent and strengthen the linkage between NATO's conventional forces and United States intercontinental strategic systems; and by augmenting NATO long-range theatre nuclear forces, close a gap in the spectrum of escalation and provide increased options for restrained and controlled responses. An upward adjustment in long-range theatre nuclear forces would minimise the risk that the Soviets might believe — however incorrectly — that they could use long-range forces to make or threaten limited strikes against NATO Europe from locations deep in the Soviet Union. Ministers agreed that conventional force requirements should continue to take priority in force planning and that there would be no question of NATO increasing its reliance on nuclear

weapons or of lowering the nuclear threshold.[39]

Finally, on 12 December 1979, a special meeting of foreign ministers and ministers of defence of twelve NATO countries 'concluded that the overall interest of the Alliance would best be served by pursuing two parallel and complementary approaches of TNF modernisation and arms control'.[40] Accordingly it was decided to deploy 572 US systems in Europe, as shown in the accompanying table. The twin

	'Pershing' II *(1,800 km.)*	*GLCM* *(2,500 km.)*
West Germany	108	96
United Kingdom		160
Italy		112
Belgium		48
Netherlands		48
Totals	108	464
Grand total	572	

decisions on modernisation and arms control were agreed upon by all participating countries. Two countries, Belgium and the Netherlands, while accepting the overall decisions, made some reservations about the planned deployment of GLCMs on their soil. Development and production of the new missiles were not mentioned in the communiqué, because these were considered to be a US responsibility. The deployment will be spread over several years. It is scheduled to begin in December 1983 and should be completed by 1988.

The 'Pershing' II will replace the ageing shorter-range 'Pershing' I and will use its infrastructure. The GLCMs are entirely new. They and the 'Pershings' will have sufficient range (2,500 and 1,800 km. respectively) to reach targets in the Soviet Union. Such a range was considered essential to counteract the combined effects of a growing Soviet armoury targeted specifically against Western Europe and the decreas-

39. Communiqué, 14 November 1979.
40. Communiqué, 12 December 1979.

ing vulnerability of the Soviet Union itself as the result of its improved air defences. Through their capability to reach the Soviet Union itself, the new systems will clearly demonstrate the American willingness to involve superpower territory when necessary to counter threats against Western Europe. In this respect it is also important that the new systems will be stationed on the European continent itself. This offers a stronger and more visible reaffirmation of the US commitment than would have been provided by sea-based systems.

The LRTNF modernisation is designed to offset but not to match the new Soviet systems. Even after modernisation has been completed, the Soviet Union will still maintain a lead, although a reduced one. The comparative moderation of the NATO response can be measured by the fact that the whole modernisation programme will, when completed in 1988, involve only about half as many warheads (572) as the SS–20 programme alone (namely 351 × 3 = 1,053 warheads).

It has been contended that, in view of their accuracy and location, the new systems would pose a first strike threat to the Soviet Union. The facts in no way bear this out. Cruise missiles fly at subsonic speed (mach 0.9) and would need about 2 hours to reach their traget. They are thus quite unsuited for a surprise attack. The 108 'Pershings' cannot possibly be seen as a serious menace to the Soviet Union's far more numerous theatre systems and its 2,500 strategic systems, most of which are beyond the reach of the 'Pershings' anyway. In reality, the Soviets have a far greater counter-force potential in the European theatre than NATO.

The Alliance stressed that the modernisation will not increase its reliance on nuclear weapons or in any way alter its strategy of deterrence. In fact, the special meeting on 12 December 1979 decided on the withdrawal of 1,000 US warheads from Europe as a unilateral gesture, parallelling Brezhnev's announcement in October that some troops and tanks would be withdrawn from East Germany (see p. 73). The warheads were removed in 1980, thus bringing the nuclear stockpile in Europe down from 7,000 to 6,000 warheads. It was agreed in addition that for each new warhead introduced in the course of the modernisation, another warhead would be withdrawn from the existing stockpile. The reduction of 1,000 warheads and the subsequent accommodation of new LRTNF warheads within the reduced level imply a numerical shift from warheads for shorter-range delivery vehicles to warheads for the longer-range vehicles. The High Level Group examines how these adjustments can best be made in conjunction with an overall review of NATO's TNF requirements for deterrence. A first report concluded that the 'Nike/Hercules', a dual-capable medium- and high-altitude air defence missile, could be replaced by an improved conventional system. It is also expected that when 'Atomic Demolition Munitions', a nuclear device designed to create artificial obstacles that hamper enemy mobility, reach the end of their useful life time, conventional replacement would be available.

Concurrently with the modernisation decision, NATO offered to start negotiations immediately with the Soviet Union on limiting theatre nuclear systems (the arms control 'track'). The aim of these talks, to be held between the United States and the Soviet Union, would be to bring about a more balanced situation at the lowest possible level. The December 1979 communiqué enumerated the following principles, which had been worked out in the Special Group:

(*a*) Any future limitations on US systems principally designed for theatre missions should be accompanied by appropriate limitations on Soviet theatre systems.

(*b*) Limitations on US' and Soviet long-range theatre nuclear systems should be negotiated bilaterally in the SALT III framework in a step-by-step approach.

(*c*) The immediate objective of these negotiations should be the establishment of agreed limitations on US and Soviet land-based long-range theatre nuclear missile systems.

(*d*) Any agreed limitations on these systems must be consistent with the principle of equality between the sides. Therefore, the limitations should take the form of *de jure* equality both in ceilings and in rights.

(*e*) Any agreed limitations must be adequately verifiable.

The deeper the cuts in the Soviet arsenal that could be agreed upon, the greater the part of NATO's modernisation programme that could be cancelled. Later, NATO was to take this position to its logical conclusion, proposing that there should be no LRTNF missiles on either side (the so-called 'zero-option').

Before the two-track decision was taken, it was debated — with great intensity in some NATO countries — whether negotiations should precede rather than accompany modernisation. Everything should be tried to prevent a new round in the arms race, and it was considered by some that the chances of achieving this would be better if the modernisation decision were postponed. The Special Group did examine the possibility, but concluded that without a modernisation decision the Soviet Union would lack the incentive to come to an agreement. If the United States came empty-handed to the negotiations, it would have no leverage for inducing the Soviet Union to make substantial cuts in the new systems it had been fielding. In fact the Soviets would be encouraged to drag on the negotiations if they were given reason to believe that modernisation could thus be postponed indefinitely. The US Assistant Secretary of State for European Affairs, George S. Vest, summarised the reasons for not delaying the decision:

> 'There are those, I know, who argue that NATO should delay its deployment decision until such talks can be held. We must not delay — for two important reasons.
>
> 'First, we cannot know in advance that such talks will succeed. It would make little sense for the Allies to fall farther and farther behind in the mere hope that the talks might succeed. And given the present momentum of Soviet efforts, any delay in NATO modernisation increases an already troubling disparity.
>
> 'Second, the West must demonstrate its seriousness about modernization — or the Soviets will have no visible incentive to negotiate reductions in forces.'[41]

Since the first new US systems would not be ready before the end of 1983, there was and still is sufficient time to reach an agreement on mutual limitations before any actual deployments take place on the Western side.

---

41. The speech was prepared for the US Secretary of State, Cyrus Vance, but delivered by his Assistant Secretary for European Affairs in Berlin, on 10 December 1979.

The Soviet campaign against the presence of American nuclear weapons in Europe

Driving a wedge between the United States and its Allies, and ultimately bringing about the removal of US power from Europe, is a long-standing aim of Soviet foreign policy. So it was to be expected that, as soon as it became clear that NATO was heading towards the modernisation of its LRTNF, the Soviet Union would launch a broad range of activities, both overt and covert, to try and keep European countries from accepting the new missiles on their soil.

The Soviet campaign against the neutron bomb, which had been initiated in 1977, showed that it was possible to influence NATO decisions on defence. By a combination of direct propaganda and indirect subversive actions through the medium of national communist parties and front organisations, the Soviet Union had tried to fuel the fear which the idea of a nuclear war naturally inspires in the population of Western Europe and to channel sincerely-felt religious and other objections against nuclear weapons into concrete political action. Especially in smaller NATO countries, members of communist parties had set up 'Stop the Neutron Bomb' pressure groups of a broad composition, which proved effective in influencing democratic decision-making.

A similar campaign on an even broader scale was launched by the Soviet Union against LRTNF modernisation. The renewed Soviet efforts to influence NATO decision-making on defence benefited from the greater sensitivity of the West European public to nuclear issues following the neutron bomb debate and the momentum gained by peace movements in several countries. These factors were partly neutralised by the greater consensus among traditional security élites on the need to modernise LRTNF compared with their views on the neutron bomb issue, a wide recognition that the Soviet Union had modernised first, and above all NATO's willingness to forgo modernisation in a mutual zero-option.

The fact that the Soviet Union does everything in its power to stimulate anti-nuclear and other peace movements should not cause one to overlook the genuine and authentic concern which underlies most of the present-day peace movements in the West. In this connection it is interesting to note that many of the Soviet propaganda themes against American military programmes are simply borrowed from *Western* peace research and peace movements. Many of these themes are in fact quite foreign to Soviet military thought, as described in Chapter 3. By echoing in its propaganda typically Western concerns, the Soviet Union does of course reinforce the belief in their validity among sections of the Western public.

Disarmament has long been a favourite area of Soviet propaganda, as the continuing stream of largely declaratory proposals presented by the Soviet Union in the United Nations and elsewhere attests. These tactics are being used abundantly in the TNF debate. Both before and after the modernisation decision, Brezhnev launched 'peace offensives' consisting of arms control proposals designed to project a 'peace-loving' image, in contrast to that of the American 'warmongers'. These proposals purported in fact to block NATO's modernisation programme, without establishing in return any real limitations on the growing Soviet arsenal, as will be seen in the last section.

Positions of Western protagonists

The United States. In contrast to its vacillating attitude towards the neutron bomb, the Carter administration came down strongly in favour of strengthening LRTNF and did its best to convince the Europeans of the necessity for a decision to that effect. On the eve of the special NATO meeting in December 1979, US Assistant Secretary of State Vest advocated modernisation as follows:

'It is crucial that the Soviets not be tempted to believe — however wrongly — that strategic parity between the superpowers means that Europe's defence could be separated from that of the United States, or that the Soviet Union itself could remain immune from a military conflict in Europe. Thus, deterrence requires that NATO have a full range of capabilities to respond to any level of military challenge. It requires that there be no gap in this continuum of forces: that every stone in the arch of deterrence be sound. Such a gap could emerge if we should fail to modernise NATO's long-range theatre nuclear forces. For the Soviet Union, having achieved strategic parity, appears now to be driving toward nuclear preponderance in the European theatre.

'We can see the evidence in the Soviet Union's vigorous programme to modernise and expand its long-range theatre nuclear forces. The most dramatic development in this regard — and the matter of greatest concern to us — is the rapid, ongoing Soviet deployment of the SS–20 mobile missile.'[42]

The Reagan administration followed the same course and continued to urge the Europeans to accept the new missiles on their soil:

'To form a bridge to America's strategic forces, the Alliance must implement the December 1979 decision to modernise its theatre nuclear forces. The placement of modernised US nuclear systems in Europe is a response to Allied concerns that the Soviet Union is creating the means to devastate or intimidate Europe with theatre nuclear weapons, while holding the US at bay with its strategic forces. TNF modernisation will end Soviet hopes of regionalising a nuclear conflict based on an ability to strike at the European Allies from a Russian sanctuary.

'The central idea behind TNF modernisation — like that behind the maintenance of 300,000 American soldiers in Europe — is to remove any doubt the Soviets might have about the US strategic commitment to NATO'.[43]

Great Britain.   The Conservative cabinet under Margaret Thatcher has remained, throughout the TNF debate, a staunch supporter of modernisation. The British position was summarised unequivocally by the Defence Secretary, Francis Pym, before Parliament on 13 December 1979:

'The British Government fully supported the Alliance

42. See footnote 41.
43. See footnote 36.

effort to reach agreement on this programme, which I believe is essential if we are to avoid a dangerous gap emerging in NATO's theatre nuclear capability. Such a gap would weaken the alliance's strategy of flexible response and so cast doubt on the credibility of our deterrent.

'The decision reached yesterday is a dramatic reaffirmation of the American commitment to the defence of Europe. This decision is also a demonstration of the cohesion and political will of the alliance to respond to a growing Soviet threat and to resist a massive Soviet propaganda campaign.'

Only the left wing of the Labour Party opposed the Government's stand at the time. Since then the anti-nuclear movement, which was strong in the early 1960s, has undergone a revival and now Labour and, with some qualifications, the Liberals oppose modernisation. The Social Democrats support the two-track approach.

In addition, the Thatcher Government decided that the 'Polaris' fleet would be replaced in the 1990s by 'Trident' submarines — also of American design. Opposition parties are against the project either because they consider it too expensive or because they see no need to maintain a national nuclear deterrent.

Italy. The Cossiga government agreed in autumn 1979 to receive a share of the new missiles, thus making Italy the first continental country to do so. It also fully supported the two-track decision. Subsequent governments — traditionally containing a majority of Christian Democrats — reaffirmed this position.

The Communists were the only major party to oppose the decision in December 1979: they proposed that it be postponed for six months and that negotiations be started at once. Furthermore they invited the Soviet Union to halt SS–20 production and deployment — a unique position among Communist parties. In 1981 the Communist Party joined the protest of smaller leftist groups against Italian participation in the modernisation programme.

West Germany. The former Chancellor, Helmut Schmidt, was one of the first to call attention to the growing nuclear disparities in the European theatre. He was also one of the first to stress the need to try and redress this imbalance along two parallel tracks: modernisation *and* arms control. A specific element of Germany's position was that it did not want to be the only non-nuclear country where new missiles would be stationed, a condition which was overcome thanks to Italy.

During the congress of the Social-Democratic Party (SPD) on 3–7 December 1979, Defence Minister Hans Apel described the German aims in the discussions leading up to the two-track decision:

— The decision must be supported politically by all NATO Allies;
— the production of the new weapons is a matter for the United States alone; the stationing of these weapons in Europe should be decided upon at the same time;
— the territory of the Federal Republic of Germany may not play any special role with regard to the stationing of the new weapons; its status as a non-nuclear power may not be in doubt;
— the decision should be coupled with a detailed arms control offer to the Soviet Union, to be presented without delay and aimed at the removal of the present disparity.[44]

In 1981 anti-nuclear sentiments showed a marked increase in Germany and opposition to modernisation grew within both government parties, the Social Democrats and to a lesser extend the Free Democrats (Liberals). This prompted Chancellor Helmut Schmidt and the Foreign Minister Hans-Dietrich Genscher (leader of the Free Democrats) to stake their political future on the continued acceptance by their

44. Original text:
     'Der Beschluss muss von allen NATO-Partnern politisch getragen werden;
     'Die Produktion der neuen Waffen ist allein Sache der USA, ihre Stationierung in Europa ist gleichzeitig damit zu beschliessen;
     'Die Bundesrepublik Deutschland darf keine singuläre Rolle als Stationierungsgebiet für diese neuen Systemen spielen, ihr nicht-nuklearer Status darf nicht in Zweifel gezogen werden;
     'Der Beschluss ist mit einem detaillierten und unverzüglich vorzulegen Rüstungskontrollangebot an die Sowjetunion zu verbinden mit dem Ziel, die Disparitäten abzubauen.'

respective parties of the *'Doppelbeschluss'* (= decision in favour of the 'double-track'). The Christian Democrats, who returned to power in October 1982, are firm supporters of modernisation.

Belgium. TNF modernisation only became an issue in Belgium about a month before the NATO decision was taken. In November 1979 the Flemish Socialists, probably following the example of their Dutch sister-party, started opposing the NATO plans. Opposition soon spread to the Walloon Socialists and some of the linguistic parties. The Social Christians, with the exception of a few dissidents, supported the two-track approach and so did the Liberal opposition.

The coalition government of Wilfried Martens was deeply divided over the issue. On 12 December 1979, it did finally endorse the overall NATO decision, but stated that the decision on the stationing of cruise missiles on Belgian soil would be taken six months later. On 19 September 1980 — there had been a further delay due to a change in the coalition — a new compromise was reached within the Belgian government (again headed by Martens), under which the outcome of the US-Soviet negotiations was accepted in advance; if the negotiations failed, Belgium would take its allotted share of cruise missiles. The Belgian position was set out to the Alliance in the following terms:

1. If our ideal goal materialises, i.e. a ban on all medium-range missiles on both sides, we will not have to place any of them in Belgium.

2. If the final agreement only sets certain limitations, certain ceilings on the deployment of these missiles by both sides, we will agree to take the proportional share of missile deployments allotted to us.

3. If the negotiations should not yield any results, we would, in solidarity with our Allies, accept the full implementation in Belgium of our part of the task agreed among the NATO Allies.[45]

45. *La libre Belgique*, 9 September 1980. Original text:
'1. Si notre objectif idéal se réalise, c'est-à-dire une suppression de part et d'autre de toutes les fusées à portée moyenne, nous n'auront pas à en placer en Belgique.

Subsequent coalitions reaffirmed this stand.

The Netherlands.   The successful 'Stop the Neutron Bomb' campaign in 1977–8 contributed to the negative stance of the Dutch government on the issue and gave the Dutch peace movement fresh impetus. In 1979 the movement started campaigning against NATO's modernisation plans. It reached its peak in the autumn of 1981 and receded somewhat in 1982. Because the movement is composed of both leftist and religious strands, its influence was felt in a large part of the Dutch political system: the whole left and a minority within the Christian Democrat centre oppose modernisation. Only the Liberals on the right explicitly support the modernisation track. In the period leading up to the NATO decision, the Christian Democrat Prime Minister Andreas van Agt had to steer a difficult middle course between the Atlantic orientation of his Liberal coalition partner and the strong opposition to modernisation in Parliament, by some members of his own party among others. The result was that on 12 December 1979 the Netherlands announced a two-year postponement of the decision regarding the stationing of cruise missiles on its territory:

> 'The Netherlands agrees that there is a need for a political and military answer to threatening developments in relation to Soviet LRTNF, particularly the SS–20 missile and the 'Backfire' bomber. In view of the importance we attach to arms control and to the 'zero-option' as the ultimate objective in the long-range theatre nuclear field, the Netherlands cannot yet commit itself to the stationing of ground-launched cruise missiles on its territory.
>
> 'The Netherlands will take a decision in December 1981, in consultation with the Allies, on the basis of the criterion

'2. Si l'accord final établit seulement certaines limites, certains plafonds pour le déploiement de ces fusées de part et d'autre, nous accepterons de prendre proportionnellement la part qui nous reviendra des fusées à déployer.

'3. Si les négociations n'aboutissaient pas, nous accepterions en solidarité avec nos Alliés l'exécution intégrale en Belgique de notre part de la mission adoptée entre partenaires de l'OTAN.'

whether or not arms control negotiations have by then achieved success in the form of concrete results.'[46]

By December 1981, when the decision was due, a centre-left coalition, headed again by van Agt, had been formed. It included the Labour Party, which opposes not only the stationing of new missiles on Dutch territory but the modernisation decision as a whole. The most the coalition partners could agree upon was a new postponement of the decision. In November 1982 a centre-right coalition came to power again, which allows certain practical preparations for the stationing of GLCMs, with a view to strengthening the US hand in the negotiations.

The other NATO countries participating in the integrated military structure, though less directly concerned, endorsed the two-track decision. Denmark initially proposed delaying the decision by six months, but in the end it joined the consensus.

France — Valéry Giscard d'Estaing was then still President — did not officially take part in the decision but tacitly approved it. President Mitterrand relinquished the formal aloofness of his predecessor and openly supported modernisation. In Greece the formation of a socialist government, led by Andreas Papandreou, in October 1981 put an end to Greek political support for modernisation. But although it no longer recognises the need for modernisation, Greece does not actively oppose the programme.

The arms control track

The negotiations between the United States and the Soviet Union on the limitation of certain of their theatre nuclear systems started in Geneva on 30 November 1981. Preliminary talks had already been held from 17 October to 17 November 1980.

The term 'Intermediate-Range Nuclear Forces' (INF), freshly coined in Washington, gives the most apt description

46. Statement by the Netherlands Defence Minister, Willem Scholten, in the special meeting, 12 December 1979.

of the subject-matter of the negotiations as the West sees it. The Soviets use the term 'medium-range', a concept which roughly subsumes the same weapons as 'long-range TNF' does in Western military jargon (or 'longer-range INF' in the new terminology). 'Medium-range' systems are described as those with a range/combat radius which is less than intercontinental, but more than 1,000 km. However, there seem to be some inconsistencies, since a heavy fighter-bomber like the 'Fencer', which has a combat radius of about 1,700 km., is never mentioned in Soviet writings on 'medium-range' systems.

The present Geneva talks had their origin at the end of 1978 and beginning of 1979. That period saw the emergence of the idea that LRTNF modernisation plans, which were beginning to take shape, should be coupled with an arms control offer. This led to the establishment by the Alliance in April 1979 of a 'Special Group', which worked out a negotiating framework, summarised in the communiqué of 12 December 1979 (see p. 92).

In the course of 1979 the Soviet campaign to thwart NATO's modernisation plans also got under way. Arms control proposals were going to play an increasingly important role in this campaign. The speech made by Brezhnev in Berlin on 6 October 1979 sounded the start of a major 'peace offensive'. This speech, which set the pattern for the whole subsequent propaganda campaign, alternated veiled threats with attempts to cajole the Western public into refusing the new missiles on their soil through references to a possible reduction in the number of medium-range systems in the Western parts of the Soviet Union. (The following extract is in the Tass translation.)

> 'Realisation of NATO's plans would inevitably aggravate the situation in Europe and vitiate in many respects the international atmosphere in general. It is no secret that the Federal Republic of Germany, alongside of the USA, is assigned not the least part in the preparation of these dangerous plans. Frankly speaking, those who shape the policy of that country are facing today a very serious choice. They will have to decide which is best for the FRG: to help strengthen peace in Europe and develop peaceful,

mutually beneficial co-operation among European states [. . .] or to contribute to a new aggravation of the situation in Europe and the world by deploying in its territory American missile nuclear arms spearheaded against the USSR and its Allies. It is clear that in this latter case the position of the FRG would considerably worsen. *It is not hard to see what consequences the FRG would have in store for itself if these new weapons were put to use by their owners one day.*

'The above said also applies, of course, to other European NATO countries which would be 'lucky' enough to have American medium-range missile nuclear arms deployed in their territories.

'As for the Soviet Union I repeat again and again that we do not seek military superiority. [. . .] Our strategic doctrine is purely defensive in nature. [. . .] I will say more. *We are prepared to reduce the number of medium-range nuclear means deployed in Western areas of the Soviet Union as compared to the present level but, of course, only in the event if no additional medium-range nuclear means are deployed in Western Europe.* I also want to confirm solemnly that the Soviet Union will never use nuclear arms against those states that renounce the production and acquisition of such arms and do not have them on their territory . . .

'Lying ahead, as is known, are also important talks on SALT III. We are for commencing them immediately after the entry into force of the SALT II treaty. Within the framework of these talks we agree to discuss the possibilities of limiting not only intercontinental but also other types of armaments, but with due account, of course, for all related factors and strict observance of the principle of the equal security of the sides.'

It was in this speech that Brezhnev also announced the unilateral withdrawal of 20,000 Soviet troops and 1,000 tanks from East Germany, as was discussed under the MBFR heading.

The proposal to reduce the level of medium-range systems was formulated in such a way as to leave open the possibility of making good the offer merely by retiring some of the ageing bombers or missiles or by moving them east of the Urals. NATO, on the other hand, would have had to give up its modernisation plans and acquiesce in the growing imbalance created by the Soviet deployment of SS–20s, 'Backfires' etc., which would be allowed to continue unimpeded.

In November, the Soviet authorities stepped up the pressure: if NATO persisted in its modernisation plans, the basis for arms control negotiations would be destroyed. This theme was first broached by the Soviet Foreign Minister, Andrei Gromyko, during a press conference on 23 November 1979, following an official visit to Bonn:

> 'If the decision [to modernize] were taken, if our proposal to start negotiations immediately were declined, then the position of the Western side will have destroyed the basis for negotiations. Negotiations cannot take place, if certain countries seek their luck in a new arms race.'

On 18 December 1979 — six days after the special NATO meeting — the United States offered to start talks with the Soviet Union on INF. However, the Soviet Union demanded that the modernisation decision should first be reversed. The Soviets maintained this unacceptable precondition until the visit of the West German Chancellor, Helmut Schmidt, to Moscow on 30 June–1 July 1980 when

> The Soviet side, guided by the broad interests of peace and security, proposed that a start be made on discussing the matter of medium-range nuclear missile weapons simultaneously and linked organically with the matter of American forward-based nuclear weapons.[47]

The Soviet Union was now willing to negotiate too, but it still differed widely from the West on the subject-matter of the talks. NATO envisaged the negotiations as a step-by-step process (see p. 92, the 12 December 1979 communiqué). The first step should focus on land-based missiles, because it is in that field that the most dynamic and destabilizing developments are taking place, namely the SS–20 deployments. Subse-

47. Joint Party-Government statement, 4 July 1980.

quent steps could then broaden the scope of the limitations.

Concentrating in the first instance on a limited set of weapons will simplify the task of the negotiators and thus make early agreement easier. This is important because the number of SS–20s continues to increase and, from December 1983 onwards, deployments will begin on the NATO side too. If the negotiators had to tackle a wide array of weaponry including aircraft and sea-based systems simultaneously, as the Soviets propose, they would be faced with an enormously complicated task which would undoubtedly take much longer to resolve. In the Soviet view, the negotiations should cover right from the start both 'medium-range' systems and American 'Forward-Based Systems', a concept which had already been put forward in SALT (see pp. 66–7) and was now being revived. Although the list of American FBSs has varied in the past, nowadays it generally includes:

— F-4 'Phantom' fighter-bombers,
— F-111 light bombers,
— FB-111 medium bombers,
— carrier-borne aircraft (A-6 and A-7).

Previously the list also included:

— 'Poseidon' SLBMs assigned to SACEUR,
— 'Pershing' I missiles.

FBSs are supposed to be US systems of less than intercontinental range that can nevertheless reach Soviet territory, but in fact systems that do not meet these criteria are listed as well. The combat radius of the F-4 — about 720 km. — does not allow for normal two-way missions over Soviet territory from its present locations; the same is true of the 750-km. 'Pershing' I missile. Another contradiction is that, while the Soviets only count their systems that are located in Europe, i.e. west of the Urals, they do count FB-111s and carrier aircraft which are based in the United States. The 'Poseidon' SLBMs are counted against the SALT ceilings and have therefore rightly been dropped from the FBS list.

The scope of the negotiations, as the Soviet Union sees it, is rather lop-sided. Of their arsenal only 'medium-range' systems would be involved (i.e. SS–4, SS–5 and SS–20, 'Badger', 'Blinder' and 'Backfire'). On the American side, systems with a much shorter range would be included, but not comparable Soviet systems. For example, while the F–4 would be subject to limitations, the 'Fencer', which has about double the range, would not; nor would the many other dual-capable fighter-bombers of Soviet Frontal Aviation, which have ranges similar to the F–4. It is on the basis of such selective inclusions and exclusions that the Soviets claim that a nuclear balance already exists in Europe — a balance, they argue, which would be upset by the 572 new NATO missiles. In fact, the Soviets enjoy an overwhelming nuclear superiority in Europe, even when the British and French nuclear forces are taken into account, as we saw in Chapter 4.

Preliminary talks were held in Geneva at the end of 1980, and the subsequent change of administration in Washington inevitably delayed their resumption. In the mean time Brezhnev resumed his peace offensive. Speaking on 23 February 1980 he managed, as on previous occasions, to include veiled threats:

> 'It must be clear: the deployment of new US missiles, targeted against the USSR and its allies, in the FRG, Italy, Britain, the Netherlands or Belgium, is bound to affect our relations with these countries, to say nothing of how this will prejudice their own security. So their governments and parliaments have reason to weigh the whole thing again and again.'

Along with this went a seemingly attractive arms control proposal:

> 'We suggest coming to terms that already now a moratorium should be set on the deployment in Europe of new medium-range nuclear missile weapons of the NATO countries and the Soviet Union, that is, to freeze the existing quantitative and qualitative level of these weapons, naturally including the US forward-based nuclear weapons in this region. The moratorium could enter into force at once, the moment negotiations begin on this score, and could operate until a permanent treaty is concluded on limiting or, still better, reducing such nuclear weapons in Europe. In making this proposal, we expect the two sides to

stop all preparations for the deployment of corresponding additional weapons, including US 'Pershing' II missiles and land-based strategic cruise missiles.'[48]

The moratorium proposal is another attempt to block NATO's LRTNF modernisation, without having to subject the military programmes which prompted the NATO decision to any significant limitations. It was rejected by all NATO countries. When the proposal was made, the Soviet Union had already deployed some 220 SS–20s (660 warheads) and seventy strike-configured 'Backfires', whereas the NATO programme had not yet begun. To freeze such an imbalance would have meant consecrating an unacceptable disparity. Moreover, the moratorium only covered the European part of the Soviet arsenal. Deployment of SS–20s could have continued to the east of the Urals, from where they could still easily have reached targets in Western Europe. If the freeze, which was proposed for the duration of the negotiations, had been accepted, the Soviets, having achieved their prime objective — the blocking of NATO modernisation — would have had every reason to let the talks drag on indefinitely.

Later, slightly improved variants of the moratorium were advanced, but these were only marginally less disadvantageous for the West, and in no way met the above objections. When the talks in Geneva got under way, the moratorium concept was incorporated in the Soviet opening proposals. Confronted with unanimous rejection by NATO and a sceptical reception by European public opinion, the Soviets abandoned the idea of a reciprocal moratorium. Instead, Brezhnev announced on 16 March 1982 a *unilateral* moratorium: SS–20 deployments would be halted, he said, 'in the European part of the USSR'.[49] The unilateral moratorium would last until agreement was reached in Geneva, or until 'practical preparations to deploy "Pershing" II and cruise missiles' had begun. The impact on Western public opinion, at which the move was clearly aimed, remained very limited because US intelligence on the SS–20 programme, which has

48. Address to the XXVI Congress of the Communist Party, translation from *Moscow News*, no. 9, 1981.
49. Address before Soviet Trade Union Congress.

proved remarkably accurate, showed that deployments were continuing uninterruptedly both east and west of the Urals — despite Brezhnev's statement and despite an even more categorical statement on 18 May.

In a speech to his military top brass on 27 October 1982, Brezhnev said that 'practical preparations' for deployment of the US missiles in Europe were under way, which, according to his previous statement, would have put an end to the SS–20 moratorium. This seemed to imply a formal termination of the fiction of a pause in SS–20 deployments, but in later declarations it appeared yet again.

The United States developed its negotiating position in the months preceding the start of the talks on 30 November 1981, in close consultation with their Allies. The consultations were conducted mainly within the 'Special Consultative Group', which had been established by the North Atlantic Council in January 1980 for the purpose of preparing and following the negotiations. The Special Consultative Group can be seen as a follow-up to the 'Special Group', which prepared the arms control track in the period leading up to the December 1979 decision.

The consultation process led to the adoption of the 'zero option', sometimes also described as the 'zero-level outcome' or the 'zero-zero solution'. According to this formula, the United States would cancel the planned deployment of 'Pershings' and GLCMs, while the Soviet Union would dismantle its SS–20 missiles and retire its SS–4 and SS–5 missiles. Realisation of the 'zero option' would be a major step forward, eliminating the weapons that cause the greatest concern to each side.

It has been pointed out that the planned 572 new missiles were necessary not only to counter the SS–20 but also, more generally, to reaffirm the link between Europe and America in the face of a balance which is deteriorating at both the strategic and the theatre level, including a shift in relative vulnerability due to the simultaneous growth of Soviet air strike and air defence capabilities. This in fact underscores the far-reaching nature, from an arms control perspective, of the zero option offer. Of course, NATO would not be the only side to give up something. What is required of the Soviet Union is not inconsiderable either: the dismantling of *all* their brand-new SS–20s — not just those in Europe. The forced retirement of the remaining SS–4s and SS–5s should be comparatively easy, since these missiles are nearing the end of their useful life anyway. Elimination of the SS–20s would reduce the Soviet superiority to more acceptable proportions. This would to a certain extent ease the linkage problem, which prompted the December 1979 decision.

The following are the key principles underlying the American negotiating position, as it is being expounded in Geneva:

Phased negotiations.   To try and negotiate at one and the same time about all Intermediate-Range Nuclear Forces would be impossibly complicated. Dealing first with a clearly defined and limited category of relatively comparable systems increases the chances for early agreement. Initial success would lay the foundations for broadening the scope of the negotiations in subsequent phases.

Initial focus on land-based missiles.   Each side considers the land-based missiles of the other side, especially the ballistic ones, as the most serious threat. As SS–20 deployments continue, the threat to NATO in this respect is steadily increasing. The Soviet Union for its part has made clear that it attaches great importance to preventing the deployment of US land-based cruise and 'Pershing' missiles in Western Europe. These are good reasons for dealing with land-based INF missiles first.

Militarily significant reductions.   To have any military significance, an agreement has to reduce the threat. To achieve this, the weapon systems considered most threatening will have to be dismantled. A mere redeployment (east of the Urals), or the destruction of only obsolete systems which are due for replacement anyway, would hardly improve Western security. The United States proposes that longer-range INF missiles be eliminated *completely* on both sides.

Global approach.   When mobile systems with ranges of several thousands of kilometres are involved, regional limitations have no military significance. SS–20s based well to the east of the Urals could still strike at a large part of NATO Europe, and even those in the Far Eastern part of the Soviet Union could readily be moved to within range of NATO Europe. The United States therefore seeks global limitations. Naturally, not only Soviet but American options as well would be curtailed on a world-wide basis.

Equal limitations and equal rights.   These principles, sometimes also referred to as '*de jure* equality', have of course already been applied in many other arms control forums. They are closely related to the more general principles of balance and reciprocity set out on p. 62, above. The Soviet Union prefers the formulation 'equality and equal security', but it does not dispute the substance of the concept, which found a practical application in the SALT II ceilings. However, when applied to INF, an important difference appears. The United States considers that the two superpowers should be equal; while for the Soviet Union equality means that it should be allowed the same number of weapons as the United States, Britain and France taken together.

Non-circumvention.   In an agreement on the complete elimination of all land-based longer-range INF missiles, provisions to prevent circumvention will be needed. For instance, a missile like the SS–22, with its range of about 900 km., could under certain circumstances cover much the same targets as the SS–20. If an agreement on the elimination of all longer-range INF missiles is not to be undermined, such problems will have to be dealt with.

Verification.   Any limitations agreed upon should be adequately verifiable. The Soviet Union accepts the principle, but divergences over its practical applications are to be expected, as experience in other arms control forums shows.

START framework.   Reflecting the strategic unity of the Alliance, the United States sees the INF negotiations as taking place in the framework of SALT/START.

US and Soviet systems only. There are only two parties sitting at the table in Geneva: the United States and the Soviet Union. They cannot undertake any commitments for the independent nuclear forces of Britain or France. In fact, both Britain and France have made it quite clear that, in view of the comparatively very small size of their nuclear forces and of the strategic role which they ascribe them, they see no possibility of themselves participating in the arms control process between the two superpowers. Acceding to a Soviet request for compensation for the existence of Third Country forces is considered by the United States as contrary to the equality principle, since it would thereby be allowed less forces than the Soviet Union.

The Soviets rejected the zero-zero solution, accusing the United States of demanding unilateral reductions. Their own opening proposals have been described in considerable detail:

— In keeping with the principle of equality and equal security, the agreement must cover and take account of all medium-range nuclear weapons, i.e. with a range (the combat radius) of action of 1,000 km. and more deployed in Europe and in the adjacent waters or intended for use in Europe;
— With a view to a maximum reduction in the level of the above-mentioned means on both the NATO side and the Soviet side, the agreement should provide for a reduction in their present number (approximately 1,000 units on each side) to 300 units on each side by the close of 1990 with the establishment of an intermediate level of 600 units by the end of 1985;
— The sides will have the right to determine themselves the composition of the armaments to be reduced and, within the limits of the agreed reduced levels, to carry out, at their own discretion, replacement and modernization of armaments, whose framework is to be determined additionally;
— The main means for the reduction of medium-range armaments will be their destruction, which does not exclude the possibility of withdrawing a part of the armaments behind agreed lines;

— Provisions will be worked out assuring adequate control over the compliance with the commitments under the prospective agreement;
— For the period of the negotiations the sides will abstain from deploying in Europe new medium-range nuclear armaments. The medium-range armaments of the sides already deployed in this region are to be frozen both quantitatively and qualitatively.[50]

In an interview a few months later, the Soviet Defence Minister, Marshal Dmitri Ustinov, revealed some further details, indicating also that the original rather lengthy time-frame to reach the ceiling of 300 had been shortened:

In Geneva the Soviet Union made proposals providing for the creation of a vast European zone of the reduction and limitation of nuclear arms from the Arctic Ocean to Africa, from the mid-Atlantic to the Urals. It is proposed to reduce within this zone the existing medium-range nuclear weapons (with a range of 1,000 kilometres and up, but not intercontinental ones), so that after five years of this agreement the USSR and NATO would have not more than 300 units of weapons of this class each. All types of medium-range nuclear weapons would be subject to reduction — both missiles and planes. It would be prohibited to deploy in the zone nuclear weapons of new types, including, of course, both American 'Pershing' II missiles and cruise missiles.

The Soviet proposals do not provide for any commitments for third countries. But taken into account in the aggregate level of 300 units of medium-range weapons, along with the American ones, are also the missiles and planes of Britain and France. The Soviet Union cannot ignore the fact that these arms are a part of the medium-range nuclear weapons of NATO countries. They are targeted against the USSR and its allies.[51]

The Soviet proposals are based on a lop-sided definition of

50. 'A new Spiral of the Arms Race: to be or not to be?'; *Pravda*, 10 February 1982 (Tass translation).
51. *Pravda*, 20 August 1982 (Tass translation).

the subject of the talks and on the claim that a balance — about 1,000 systems on each side — already exists. This claim is spurious. For instance, the Soviets count US F-4s but not their own 'Fencers', which have a superior range well above the 1,000 km. range floor they themselves proposed; they count only their systems west of the Urals, but American aircraft on both sides of the Atlantic; they count American carrier aircraft (A–6 and A–7), whose task is one not only of power projection ashore but also of sea control (the Soviet Naval Aviation, which is designed largely to combat the US carrier force, is never mentioned in this connection); and they count British and French 'medium-range' systems.

The Soviet proposal to reduce down to an ultimate level of 300 units would oblige the United States not only to forgo planned modernisation but also to remove almost all its dual-capable aircraft from Europe, because systems belonging to Britain and France — countries that do not take any part in the reductions — would use up nearly the whole allowance of 300. The British and French systems counted by the Soviets add up (using the figures from the tables on pp. 120–3) to the numbers given in the accompanying table. Thus a ceiling of

United Kingdom

'Polaris' SLBMs	64
'Vulcan' bombers[52]	56

France

MSBS (SLBMs)	80
SSBS (land-based missiles)	18
'Mirage' IV bombers	37
Total	255

300 launchers would allow the United States to retain only forty-five dual-capable aircraft in Europe. The Soviet proposal, which would force the United States to remove hundreds of bombers and fighter-bombers from the 'zone of reduction and limitation', reveals a long-standing aim of

---

52. The figure applies to the total number of 'Vulcans' in service in the first half of 1982. At present these bombers are being retired or converted. 'Tornado' fighter-bombers are replacing them. This could modify the Soviet arms control calculus.

Soviet foreign policy: the removal of American military power from Europe and the consequent break-up of political and military ties between North America and Western Europe. The limitations on their own arsenal which the Soviets offer in return are merely cosmetic. Their proposal explicitly allows replacements (see the third paragraph of the Tass quotation, p. 111), so that replacement of the SS–4 and SS–5 by the SS–20 could proceed unhampered. New systems such as the cruise and 'Pershing' missiles would, as was to be expected, be forbidden. The present number of SS–20s targeted on Western Europe — 243 — fits within the ceiling of 300. Some 'Back-fires' or older bombers would have to be moved east of the Urals, whence they could still reach Western Europe in less than half a day's flying time.

The fact that the Soviet 'reduction' proposal allows an SS–20 force of 243 in Europe alone, (or even more if it chose), which amounts to 729 warheads, illustrates one of the flaws of the proposal: it limits only launchers, whereas warheads are a better measure of military capability. The moratorium has been incorporated into the Soviet proposals, as can be seen from the last paragraph of the Tass quotation (p. 112).

The Soviet Union's opening proposals were rejected by the United States, just as the zero solution had been rejected by the Soviet Union.

On 21 December 1982, Yuri Andropov revealed a modification of the Soviet stance:

> 'We are prepared, among other things, to agree that the Soviet Union should retain in Europe only as many missiles as are kept there by Britain and France — and not a single one more. This means that the Soviet Union would reduce hundreds of missiles, including dozens of the latest missiles known in the West as SS–20. In the case of the USSR and the USA this would be a really honest "zero-option" as regards medium-range missiles. And if, later, the number of British and French missiles were scaled down, the number of Soviet ones would be additionally reduced by as many.
>
> 'Along with this there must also be an accord on reducing to equal levels on both sides the number of medium-range

nuclear delivery aircraft stationed in this region by the USSR and the NATO countries.'[53]

The main new element here is that a separate ceiling on missiles is being offered, whereas previously the Soviet Union had advocated an aggregate ceiling on missiles and aircraft. This in itself is a step in the direction of the Western view that the talks should focus on missiles.

The proposal links the Soviet land-based missile force in Europe to the combined level of the British and French missiles (both land- and sea-based), which at present stands at 162. To reach this level the Soviet Union would have to retire the SS–4 and SS–5s and remove 81 SS–20s from the 'European zone of reduction'. Andropov did not specify whether the excess SS–20s would be dismantled or merely withdrawn to the east of the Urals. Neither did he mention Soviet SLBMs in the Baltic.

Along with the ceiling on missiles there should be one on air-craft too, Andropov said. This has always been the Soviet position. Since Andropov did not touch upon other aspects of the Soviet position, one can assume that these remain the same. This would imply that he is sticking to the proposal of an aggregate ceiling of 300 on missile launchers and aircraft, with the difference that a subceiling on missiles has been added within the aggregate ceiling. Thus what Andropov is really proposing is zero missiles and some forty-five aircraft on the US side, while the Soviet Union would retain 162 SS–20s in Europe alone and 100 (or as many more as it chose) in its Asian territory, as well as large numbers of aircraft. According to his proposal, most of the US TNF, providing the link with the strategic deterrent, would be removed from Europe. The British and French nuclear forces cannot possibly take over the vital function of linking the US strategic forces to the defence of Western Europe. By equating the British and French nuclear forces to Soviet LRTNF based in Europe, Andropov projects these national deterrents in a wider European role for which they were never intended. It is an irony of

53. Speech to celebrate the sixtieth anniversary of the USSR (Tass translation). The proposal had already been developed under Brezhnev's rule.

history that it should be the Soviets who have made a proposal which, had it been accepted, would have represented the first step towards the creation of an independent European nuclear force. Such a development, needless to say, they would be the last to welcome.

Like all previous Soviet proposals on INF, that made by Andropov is designed to maintain Soviet superiority over the United States in land-based longer-range INF missiles. This suggests that the Kremlin leadership has not yet given up the hope of stopping modernisation through the medium of Western public opinion, without having to accept any significant limitations on its own arsenal in return. Not before it becomes convinced that the latter is the only way to avoid deployments on the NATO side can real concessions be expected. This is unlikely to be before the end of 1983, when the first deployments will be giving tangible evidence of NATO's ability to carry through its decision despite internal and external pressures. The Alliance would then have to hold fast throughout 1983, a year many have predicted will prove to be one of the most difficult of its history.

Of course the West will have to show flexibility too. The pledge, which President Reagan gave on the eve of the talks, and which has since been repeated many times, is still applicable: 'We intend to negotiate in good faith and to go to Geneva willing to listen to and consider the proposals of our Soviet counterparts.'[54] The zero–zero proposal was not made on a take-it-or-leave-it basis. By the end of 1982, European leaders started suggesting that, if the zero solution proves difficult to realise straight away, an interim agreement should be sought as a first step towards a total ban. In fact that is exactly what it appeared that the US and Soviet negotiators in Geneva, Paul Nitze and Yuli Kvitsinskiy, had been doing in the summer of 1982. In informal talks they worked out together the outline of an agreement, allowing the Soviet Union a residual SS–20 force and the United States a reduced deployment of GLCMs.[55] However, the negotiators were not,

54. Speech at the National Press Club, 18 November 1982.

55. Details of the informal understanding reached between Nitze and Kvitsinskiy can be found *inter alia* in the *International Herald Tribune*, 22/23 January 1983.

in the end, backed by their capitals. In September 1982 Kvitsinskiy returned from Moscow with the message that the deal was off. No deployments whatsoever on the NATO side were acceptable. Since it seems unlikely that Kvitsinskiy would have gone as far as he did in the informal talks with Nitze without informing Moscow, one can assume that the Soviets later came to the conclusion that for the time being attempts at influencing Western public opinion furthered their aims better than an early deal with the United States.

Washington had some objections to the informal deal too, notably to the fact that, while the Soviet Union would retain a sizeable number of SS–20s combining speed and accuracy with a 100 per cent penetration probability, the United States would not be allowed any comparable capability in the form of 'Pershing' II missiles. The Soviets are of course eager to ban the 'Pershing' since it would put at risk their forces in Western Russia, which would form the second wave of attack in the event of war in Europe. Unlike Moscow, Washington wanted to keep the informal negotiating channel open so as to pursue the matter further. It is noteworthy that in the informal understanding the Soviet negotiator had, in contrast to his official stance, agreed to disregard the British and French systems. The US side had agreed to a fairly large SS–20 force remaining in Siberia — which will, no doubt, have elicited protests from Japan.

Zero–zero is clearly by far the best possible outcome, both from a disarmament point of view and for the security of all concerned. Few would dispute this — in the West, at least — but if the ideal result proves difficult to achieve straight away, it makes considerable sense to explore the possibility of an interim solution. The point of departure for devising any interim formula is that as long as the Soviet Union is allowed a residual number of SS–20s, the United States should be allowed a limited deployment (this is called the 'plus-plus' option). A 'zero-plus' option, as advocated by some, would mean inequality between the superpowers being accepted.

Following extensive consultations with their Allies, the United States tabled in Geneva on 29 March 1983 a proposal for an interim agreement. Under the new proposal the United States would substantially curtail its planned deployment of

'Pershing' IIs and GLCMs, provided the Soviet Union reduced the number of its warheads on corresponding missiles to an equal level on a global basis. The interim proposal is based on the same general criteria as the zero–zero proposal. These criteria are set out in detail on pp. 109–11. The most essential are equality of rights and limits, no compensation for third-country forces, global ceilings and adequate verification. In reaction to Soviet demands for the removal of virtually all American dual-capable aircraft from Europe, which would affect not only NATO's nuclear capability but its conventional capability just as much, another criterion was added to the list: no degradation of NATO's conventional defence capability. This does not imply that aircraft could never be discussed, but at this stage missiles should be the focus of the negotiations. The difference between the zero–zero proposal and the new one is that now only the partial elimination of land-based LRINF missiles is required, and this should make agreement with the Soviets easier. The entire elimination of this category of weapons remains the ultimate US negotiating goal, but Soviet acceptance of it is not a precondition to an interim agreement. Specific numbers for the ceilings which the United States are proposing have not yet been put forward. This is a matter for negotiation. Warheads (to be accurate: warheads on missiles on launchers) would be the main unit of limitation, since this is the better measure of military capability and takes into account the MIRVs of the SS–20. The military requirement, stated in December 1979, for a mix of cruise and ballistic missiles is being upheld. For example: if the parties were to reach agreement on a ceiling of, say, 300 warheads,[56] this would allow the Soviet Union 100 SS–20 missile launchers with three MIRVs each and the United States, for instance, 54 'Pershing' II missile launchers and 246 cruise missiles,[57] each with a single warhead.

The initial Soviet reaction was disappointing. Only four days after the proposal was put forward, Gromyko called a

56. The figure was mentioned in press reports, but Washington stressed that no specific numbers were envisioned yet. Figures are given here merely by way of illustration.

57. Divide by four to find the number of launchers (unlike the SS–20 and the 'Pershing' II, the US GLCM *launcher* carries four *missiles*).

special press conference at which he poured scorn on 'the so-called interim variant'. Apparently the Soviet leadership has chosen to try to put the maximum pressure on the West European governments and waits to see if they will pass the test of initial deployments. An uncompromising attitude in Geneva seems part of this strategy. So far the Soviets have hardly modified the extreme position they took at the outset of the talks. The mention of the SS–20 in Andropov's proposal is a first step towards recognition of the legitimate Western concern over this weapon, but the Soviet Union has still not clearly stated that it would be willing to dismantle any SS–20s (as opposed to withdrawing them east of the Urals), let alone a large number such as the West requires. The US starting position, which was already far less extreme than that of the Soviets, has now undergone major changes, so that the ball is now clearly in the court of the Soviet negotiators.

Agreement should be possible in the end. There is no doubt that it will require creativity as well as steadfastness, but the basic ingredients are there, and the political attention which the INF issue is receiving should help to keep up the momentum of the negotiations.

The Hague,
April 1983

APPENDIX

TABLES AND CHARTS

Table 1

Land-based systems with a nuclear role and a range below 350 km. destined for use against ground targets, mid-1982

| | Atlantic Alliance | | | | | Warsaw Pact | | | | |
	Type	i.o.c.*	Range (km.)	No. deployed World-wide	No. deployed In Europe	Type	i.o.c.*	Range (km.)	No. deployed USSR & NSWP[b]	No. deployed In Europe
Missiles	'Honest John'	1953	37	42	42	'Frog' 7	1965	70	680 & 205	482 & 205
	'Lance'	1972	120	109	97	'Scud' A &	1957	180	540 & 143	450 & 143
	(replaced					'Scud' B[c]	1965	300		
	'Honest					SS–21		130–140		
	John')					(replaces	1978			*a few*
	'Pluton' (Fr.)	1974	120	30	30	'Frog')				
Artillery	203 mm. howitzer	1962	14[a]	?	1000	203 mm. howitzer	1977	20	?	250
	155 mm. howitzer	1964	14[a]			240 mm. mortar	1978	10		

Notes

* = 'initial operational capability'. (*a*) Will be extended to 29 km. (*b*) Non-Soviet Warsaw Pact countries. (*c*) Will be replaced by SS–23, which has a range of 500 km.

Table 2

Land-based systems with a nuclear role and a range/combat radius of 350–1000 km. destined for use against ground targets, mid–1982

			Atlantic Alliance						Warsaw Pact		
					No. deployed						No. deployed	
	Type[a]	i.o.c.	Range/ Combat radius	World-wide	In Europe	Type[a]	i.o.c.	Range/ Combat radius	USSR & NSWP	In Europe[d]
Fighter-bombers	F-104[b] 'Starfighter'	1958	930	290	290	SU–7 'Fitter' A	1959	350	150 & 115	90 & 115 (= 60%)
	F-4[c] 'Phantom'	1962	880	624	198	MIG–21 'Fishbed' J/K/L/N	1970	650	400	240(= 60%)
	'Mirage' III E (Fr.)	1971	600	29	29	MIG–27 'Flogger' D/J	1971	800	550	330 (= 60%)
	'Jaguar' (Fr. and UK)	1974	750	80	80	SU–17/20 'Fitter' C/D	1974	900	650 & 35	390 & 35 (= 60%)
Missiles	'Pershing' 1 A	1962	750	180	180	SS–12 'Scaleboard'	1969	900	120	70
						SS–22 (replaces SS–12)	1978	900		*a few*
						SS–23 (replaces 'Scud')	1982	500		

Notes
(*a*) All the aircraft are technically dual-capable, but in many cases not the whole inventory is assigned a nuclear role, as some squadrons/regiments are trained solely for conventional missions. This would lower somewhat the figures on both sides. Especially the global 'Phantom'/F–16 and the NSWP figures are likely to include substantial numbers of exclusively conventional units.
(*b*) Being replaced by F–16 and 'Tornado'.
(*c*) Being replaced by F–16. The UK interceptor model is not included.
(*d*) It is assumed that about 60 per cent of Soviet Frontal Aviation faces NATO Europe.

Table 3

Land-based systems not included in SALT with a nuclear role and a range/combat radius of 1,000–5,000 km., destined for use against ground targets, mid–1982

		Atlantic Alliance				Soviet Union				
	Type	i.o.c.	Range/Combat radius (km.)	No. deployed World-wide	No. deployed In Europe	Type	i.o.c.	Range/Combat radius (km.)	No. deployed World-wide	No. deployed In Europe
Bombers	'Vulcan' B2[a] (UK)	1960	3,000	56	56	TU–16 'Badger' C/G	1955	2,800	310[d]	242 (= 78%)
	'Buccaneer' S2[a] (UK)	1962	1,500	36	36[b]	TU–22 'Blinder' B	1962	3,100	125[d]	97 (= 78%)
	'Mirage' IV A (Fr.)	1964	1,500	37	37	SU–24 'Fencer'	1974	1,700	550	330 (= 60%)
	F–111 A/E	1969	2,400	252	164	TU–26 'Backfire' B	1974	4,200	100[d]	60 (= 60%)
	FB–111A[c]	1969	2,870	63	0					
	F–16 'Fighting Falcon'	1982	1,600	312	68					
Missiles	SSBS S2/3 (Fr.)	1971	3,000	18	18	SS–4 'Sandal'	1959	1,900	265	265
						SS–5 'Skean'	1961	4,100	15	15
						SS–20	1977	4,400–5,000	315	220 (= 70%)

Notes
(a) Being replaced by 'Tornado', which has a shorter range.
(b) Excluding 24 'Buccaneers' with anti-ship mission.
(c) Under 'US Strategic Air Command'.
(d) Excluding some 270 'Badger' C/G, 40 'Blinder' A and 80 'Backfire' B with Soviet Naval Aviation for maritime strike.

Table 4

Sea-based systems not included in SALT, with a nuclear role and a land-attack capability, mid-1982

		Atlantic Alliance				Soviet Union				
			Range/ Combat	No. deployed					No. deployed	
				World-	In				World-	In
	Type	i.o.c.	radius	wide	Europe	Type	i.o.c.	Range	wide	Europe
Carrier aircraft	A–4 'Skyhawk' II	1970	1,000	95^a	0					
	A–6E 'Intruder'	1963	1,600	180^b	20^c					
	A–7E 'Corsair'	1966	900	288	48^c					
	'Super Etendard' (Fr.)	1979	900	36	36					
SLBM	'Polaris' A3 (UK)	1968	4,600	64	64					
	'MSBS M20' (Fr.)	1977	3,000	80	80	SS–N–5^d 'Serb'	1964	1,300	39	18
SLCM						SS–N–3 'Shaddock'^{e}	1962	450	316	221 (= 70%)
						SS–N–12^e	1976	550	72	50 (= 70%)
						SS–N–19^e	1981	450	44	31 (= 70%)

Notes
(a) US Marine Corps aircraft, which can be either land- or carrier–based. See also note (a), p. 121.
(b) 120 on twelve US carriers and 60 with the Marine Corps. See also note (a), p. 121.
(c) On two carriers in the Mediterranean. In addition to power projection ashore, the A–6 and A–7 have also an important anti-ship task.
(d) Only those not counted in SALT.
(e) On Soviet surface ships and submarines. Mainly anti-ship, but could also be used against land targets. Percentage fitted with a nuclear warhead unknown.

Table 5

Comparison of major systems relevant to START, mid–1982

		United States		
	Type	*No. of launchers*	*Warheads per missile*	*No. of warheads*
ICBMs	'Titan'	52	1	52
	'Minuteman' II	450	1	450
	'Minuteman' III	550	3	1,650
		1,052		2,152
SLBMs	'Poseidon'	304	10/14	± 3,270
	'Trident' I	216	8	1,728
		520		± 5,000
Bombers	B–52	570[a]	4/8	
	FB–111	63	2	
		633		

Notes
(*a*)　347 operational and 223 in deep storage.
(*b*)　Excluding 39 not counted under SALT.
(*c*)　Including Naval Aviation.

Type	No. of launchers	Warheads per missile	No. of warheads
	Soviet Union		
SS–11	570	1	570
SS–13	60	1	60
SS–17	150	4	600
SS–18	308	1/8/10	3,000
SS–19	310	1/6	1,800
	1,398		± 6,030
SS–N–5	18[b]	1	18
SS–N–6	400	1/2	400
SS–N–8	292	1/3	300
SS–N–17	12	1	12
SS–N–18	208	3/7	1,000
SS–NX–20	20	12	–
	950		± 1,730
'Bear'	105	2	
'Bison'	45	2	
'Backfire'	180[c]	4	
	356		

Sources

The sources for Tables 1–5 are the following: International Institute for Strategic Studies, *The Military Balance 1982–1983*, London, 1982; J.M. Collins, *US-Soviet Military Balance — Concepts and Capabilities 1960–1980*, New York, McGraw-Hill, 1980; *NATO and the Warsaw Pact — Force Comparisons*, official NATO publication, May 1982; Pentagon, *Soviet Military Power*, US Govt. Printing Office, 1983; The Organization of the Joint Chiefs of Staff, *US Military Posture for FY 1983*, US Govt. Printing Office; 'US/NATO and Soviet land-based LRTNF, July 1981', chart released by US Govt.

Chart 1

Extrapolated US/Soviet Strategic Force Ratios

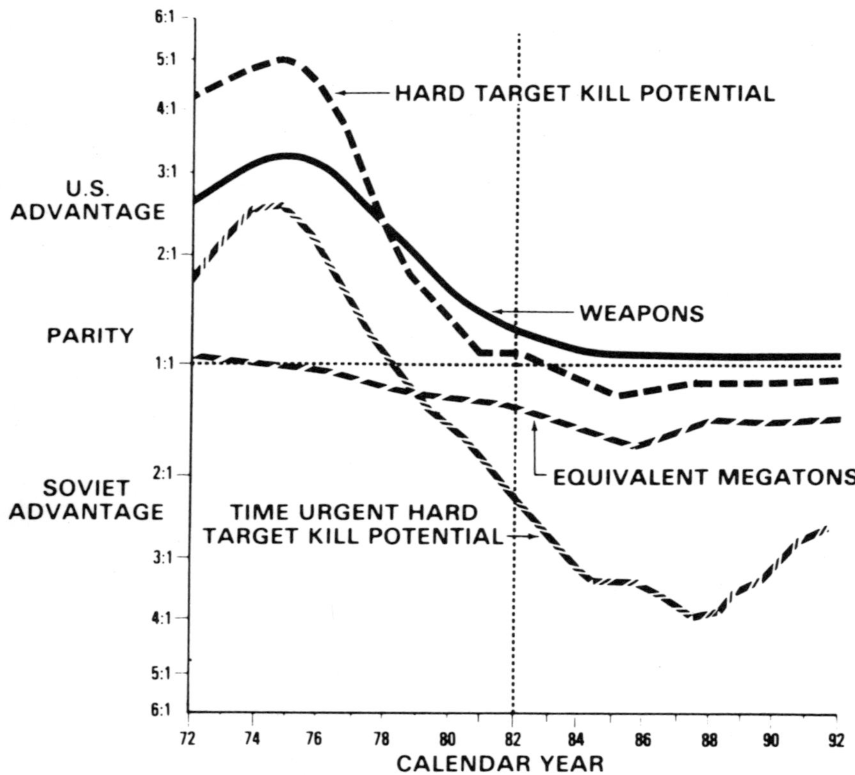

The chart is computed on the basis of total active inventories. The 'Backfire' is not included. The rapidly increasing Soviet advantage in time-urgent hard target kill potential results from the introduction of the MIRVed SS–17, SS–18 and SS–19 ICBMs (the short flight time of missiles enables them to hit time-urgent targets, i.e. targets that can be moved or launched rapidly). The difference in overall hard target kill potential is smaller, because of the US advantage in slow-flying systems (bombers and cruise missiles), which can be very accurate if they manage to get to their target.

Source: Joint Chiefs of Staff, *US Military Posture, FY 1983*, p. 23.

Chart 2

Changes in US/Soviet Strategic Levels

Source: Pentagon, *Soviet Military Power*, 2nd edn, March 1983.

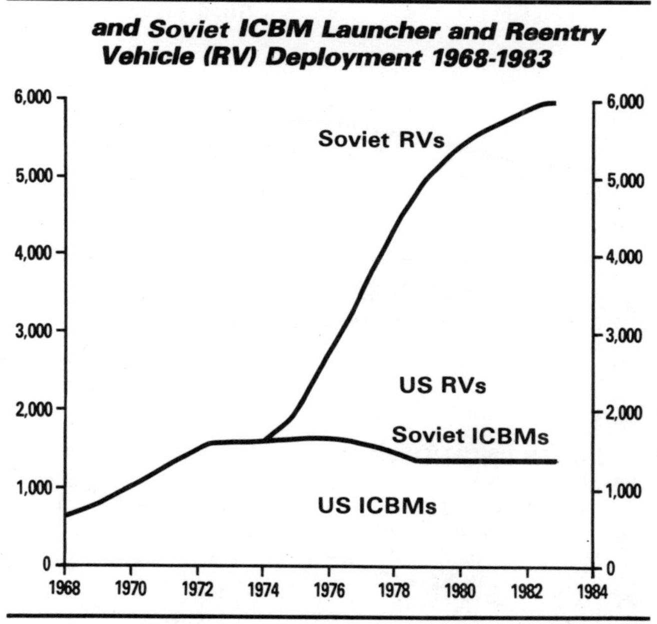

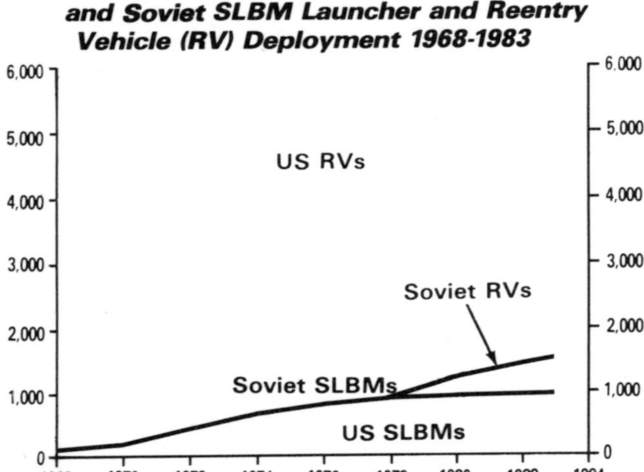

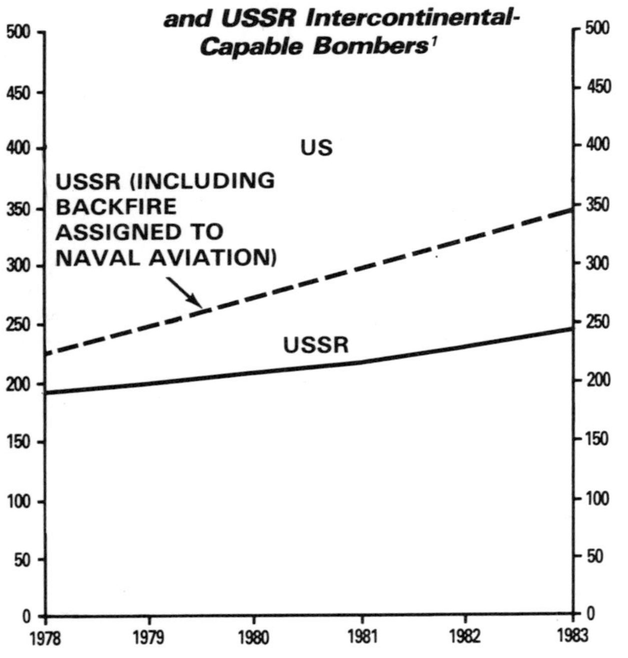

[1] US data include B-52, FB-111a ; Soviet data include Soviet Air Force BEAR, BISON, and BACKFIRE.

Chart 3

Comparison of US Defence Expenditure with Estimated Dollar Cost of Soviet Defence Activities

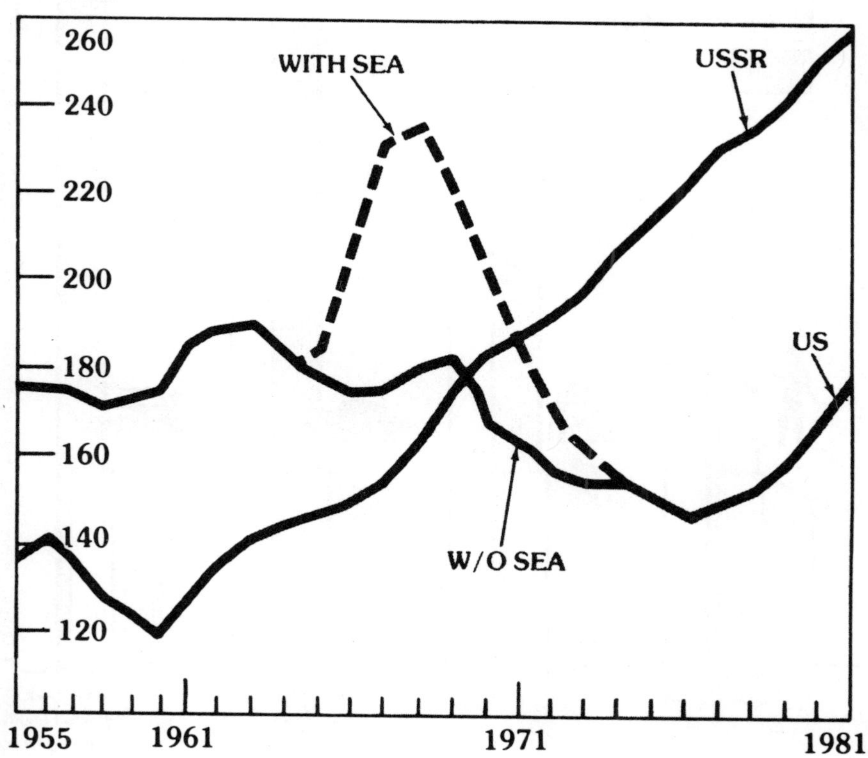

Estimating Soviet defence spending is difficult and comparing it to US defence spending even more so. The chart is based on US computations of what the Soviet defence effort would cost in the United States. These dollar-cost estimates have been criticised on the grounds that they overstate the Soviet defence effort in relation to that of the United States. But even if the inherently more conservative rouble estimates are used, the Soviet Union has still largely outspent the United States in recent years. One should bear in mind, however, that non-US NATO countries carry a share of the collective defence burden that is larger than the share carried on their side by non-Soviet Warsaw Pact countries. US figures in the chart are given with and without the expenses resulting from the war in South-East Asia.

Source: C.W. Weinberger (Secretary of Defense), *Annual Report FY 1983*, p. I–5.

Chart 4

Comparison of NATO and Warsaw Pact Conventional Forces in Europe

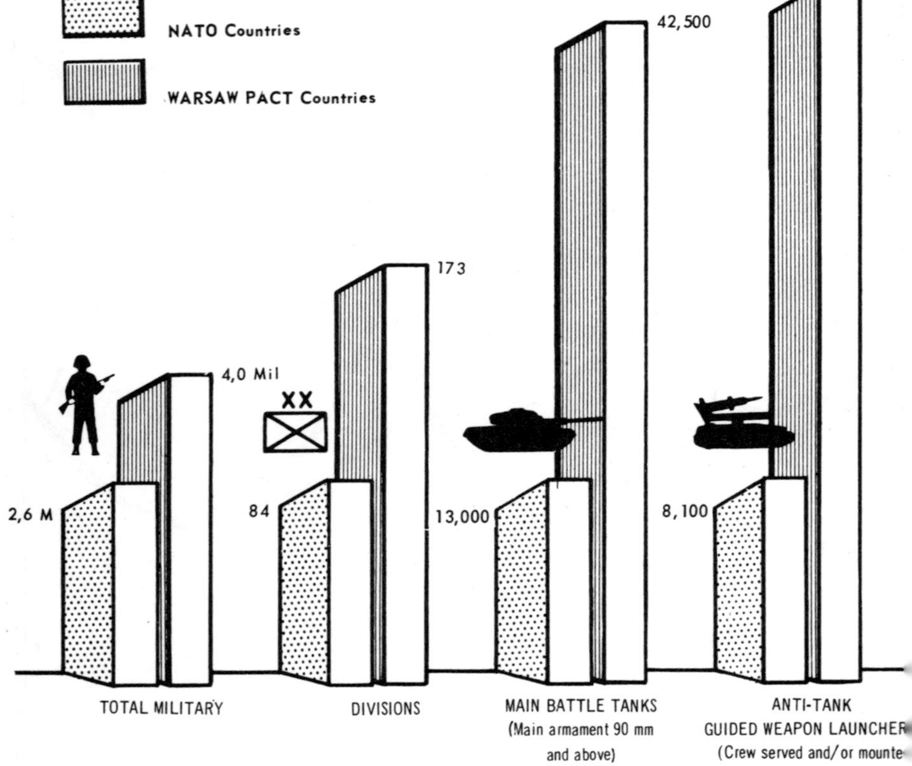

Chart 4, above, includes all in-place forces of the countries participating in NATO's integrated military structure. France is therefore excluded. The chart also excludes Spain, because the allocation of Spanish forces within the NATO Command structure has not yet been finalised. On the Warsaw Pact side, the Soviet forces in Eastern Russia (i.e. the military districts of Moscow, Volga and Ural, where the strategic reserves are located) are not counted. It should be noted that Warsaw Pact divisions normally consists of fewer personnel than many NATO divisions but contain more tanks and artillery, thereby obtaining similar combat power.

Source: NATO and the Warsaw Pact — Force Comparisons, official NATO publication, May 1982.

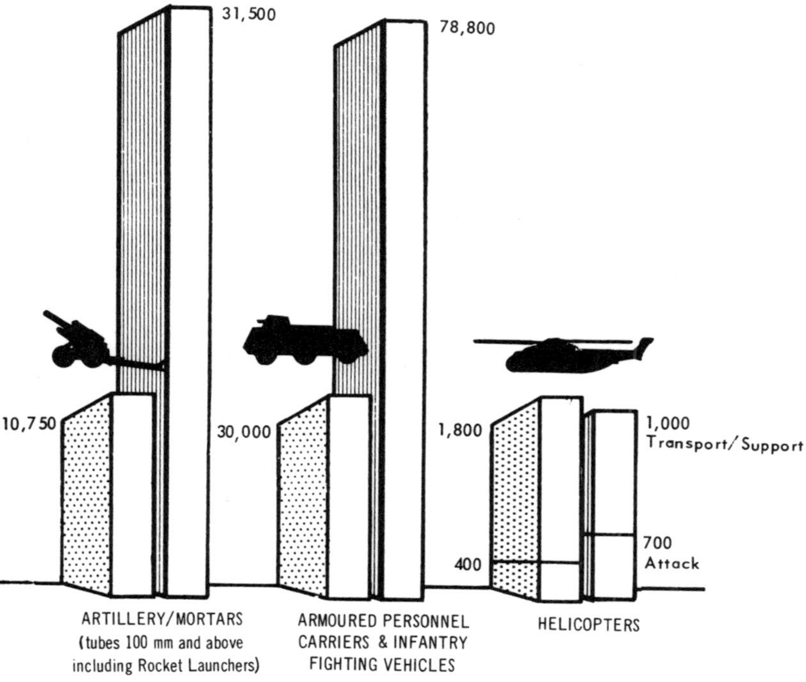

31,500
78,800
10,750
30,000
1,800
1,000
Transport/Support
400
700
Attack
ARTILLERY/MORTARS
(tubes 100 mm and above
including Rocket Launchers)
ARMOURED PERSONNEL
CARRIERS & INFANTRY
FIGHTING VEHICLES
HELICOPTERS